THE
CLASSIC
PASTA
COOKBOOK

GIULIANO HAZAN
THE
CLASSIC
PASTA
COOKBOOK

DORLING KINDERSLEY

London • New York • Stuttgart

DK

A DORLING KINDERSLEY BOOK

Project Editor
Mari Roberts

Art Editor
Tracey Clarke

Senior Editor
Carolyn Ryden

Managing Editor
Daphne Razazan

Managing Art Editor
Carole Ash

Photography
Amanda Heywood
Clive Streeter

Production
Antony Heller

A mia mamma, con tanto amore

First published in Great Britain in 1993
by Dorling Kindersley Limited,
9 Henrietta Street, London WC2E 8PS

Reprinted 1994 (Twice)

A CIP catalogue record for this book is available
from the British Library.

ISBN 0-7513-0052-7

Reproduced in Singapore by Colourscan
Printed and bound in Italy by A. Mondadori Editore, Verona

CONTENTS

MAKING AND SERVING PASTA

CLASSIC SAUCES

Easy-to-follow instructions, with a unique photographic guide to ingredients

RECIPES

Traditional and modern recipes arranged according to pasta shape

FOREWORD

It is not every day that a mother has the opportunity to introduce her son to his readers. When it happens, she should take advantage of her unique knowledge of the aptitudes and experiences that have led the author to his calling. She should start at the very beginning, which is what I propose to do.

Giuliano's passion for pasta sprang to life fully formed one day at dinner when he was three. It was the first time an adult dish of pasta had been put before him, and I well remember what it was: handmade *tortelloni* his grandmother had prepared, stuffed with *ricotta* and Swiss chard. Without ever coming up for air, he put away a portion that might have strained the capacity of a full-grown man, and as he finished he fell instantly asleep. He came out of his stupor a confirmed devotee of pasta, a devotion he has fed, and which has fed him, from that day to this.

Very early on, Giuliano's aptitude for consuming pasta began to coincide with an interest in producing it. The kitchen was his favourite playroom. He was chopping onions as soon as his hands could firmly hold a knife, and stirring sauce as soon as he was tall enough to look into the saucepan on the range. As he grew, to cook became as commonplace for him as to throw a ball was for other boys.

He would not be unwilling, I am sure, to acknowledge his debt to the Hazan kitchen, where the recipes constantly being tested provided his talents with the most favourable ground on which to develop. But the debt does not fall entirely on his side. The published form of many of those recipes owes much to his palate, often pressed into service as the official tasting instrument. To those who have not observed Giuliano at work, I can only describe his palate as possessing the gastronomic equivalent of perfect pitch.

As you look through and cook from the recipes he has set down here you will see what I mean. The judiciously balanced flavours of his sauces, his light-handed way with herbs and condiments, the illuminating pairing of sauce with the most congenial shape and type of pasta, all show an extraordinary commitment to and command of those principles of cooking whose sole aim is to produce satisfying flavour. You will never find Giuliano asking himself what he can do that is different but, rather, what he can do that tastes good.

In my life as a cook, both before it became my profession and since, I have always learned most about cooking from those who took it up out of irresistible love. This book is the product of just such love. Any cook using it will be deliciously rewarded. As a matter of fact, there are a number of things I am myself longing to try. *Bravo Giuliano!*

Marcella Hazan

INTRODUCTION

For me, few foods can compete with the satisfaction and pleasure of eating a good dish of pasta. It is difficult to imagine many Italians surviving without it. In fact, when the first Italian immigrants began arriving in the United States at the end of the 19th century, ships from southern Italy laden with pasta soon followed them. By 1913 almost 700,000 tons were being exported to the States.

Food historians have long debated the origin of pasta. Marco Polo has been attributed with discovering it in China and bringing it back to Italy in 1295, but Italian historians claim pasta was known and used in Italy before Marco Polo was even born. Sicilians say they invented it, and provide references to "macarruni" in literature as proof, while a late 19th-century Neapolitan writer, Matilde Serao, tells of a fable that attempts to designate Naples as the place where pasta made its first appearance.

She wrote that in 1220 there lived in Naples a magician called Chico. He rarely came out of his top-floor rooms except for occasional trips to the market to buy various herbs and tomatoes. (Getting tomatoes was a neat trick for Chico to pull because everybody else in Europe had to wait another 400 years, until well after Europeans first went to America.) He spent his days in front of a bubbling cauldron, and his nights poring over ancient texts and manuscripts. After many years, he achieved his goal. He rejoiced in the knowledge that he had discovered something that would contribute to the happiness of all people.

During all this time, Jovanella, whose husband worked in the kitchens of the King's palace, had been spying on Chico's every move from her balcony, which gave her a view of his rooms. When she finally discovered his secret, she told her husband, "Go tell the

King's chef that I have discovered a new food so exquisite that it deserves to be tasted by His Majesty." So her husband spoke to the chef, who spoke to the butler, who spoke to a count, who, after much deliberation, spoke to His Majesty. The King, who was getting bored with his food, welcomed the opportunity to try something different. Jovanella was admitted to the royal kitchens and began to prepare what she had seen the magician create.

She combined flour, water and eggs to form a dough, which she then painstakingly thinned out until it was as thin as parchment. She cut it into strips and formed rings, which she left out to dry. She then cooked onions, meat and tomatoes over a very low heat for a long time until they formed a sauce. When it was time to eat, she cooked the pasta in boiling water, drained it and tossed it with the sauce and "the famous cheese from Parma". The King was so impressed by what she had made that he asked her how she had managed to invent such a remarkable thing. She answered that an angel had revealed it to her in a dream. The King ordered that she be rewarded handsomely for having made such an important contribution to human happiness. One day Chico smelled the aroma of his wonderful invention coming from a nearby house. Incredulous, he asked what was being prepared. He was told of a wonderful new food which an angel had revealed to a woman in her sleep. Heartbroken, he ran off, and was never seen again.

However it may first have appeared, Italians have been making pasta for centuries. Although it has evolved into many different shapes, the basic ingredients are still the same. There are two main categories: flour-and-water pasta, and egg pasta. It is important to understand the characteristics of each.

Flour-and-water pasta uses flour made from durum (hard) wheat, a high-gluten flour called *semolina* in Italian. This category includes packeted pastas such as *spaghetti*, tubes and many special shapes. They are sturdy and work well with spicy, zesty sauces and with olive oil-based ones. This pasta is referred to as shop-bought pasta and it is best when factory-made. Industrial-strength machines are necessary to knead the hard dough, and humidity- and temperature-controlled chambers are required to dry the final shapes so they will not crack and break when cooked. I know of no brands made outside Italy that can match the quality of the Italian-made flour-and-water pastas.

The other category of pasta is made with flour and eggs and is usually referred to as homemade egg pasta or simply homemade pasta, although it is often, and inappropriately, known as "fresh pasta". It is made with a soft-wheat flour known in Italy as "00" and roughly equivalent to plain or all-purpose flour. The recipe for the dough varies slightly depending on the region. In Tuscany, for example, some olive oil and salt are added, and in Liguria a little water is used. But in Emilia-Romagna, which is known for producing the finest homemade pasta and is the birthplace of *tagliatelle, tagliolini, lasagne* and several stuffed pastas, the dough is made using only flour and eggs and nothing else (except for spinach or tomato pasta). Egg pasta is able to absorb sauces more readily than flour-and-water, shop-bought pasta, and so is well suited to butter- and cream-based sauces, and to milder sauces that match its delicate texture. With sauces where olive oil is prominent, egg pasta would absorb too much oil and become slick and gummy.

Egg pasta, unlike shop-bought pasta, should be made at home. The finest homemade pasta is porous, delicately textured and very thin, a result that can be achieved only by kneading the dough by hand and thinning it out with a rolling pin. Very good egg pasta can also be produced by rolling it through a machine if you are willing to sacrifice some of its porousness and texture. Kneading, however, should always be done by hand. The so-called "fresh" pasta found in the refrigerator compartments of supermarkets and speciality shops is egg pasta at its worst. The noodles are usually too thick, the dough is made with *semolina*, which is much too hard a flour for egg pasta, and it is refrigerated so that it can be called "fresh". Cold is pasta's greatest enemy. In fact, you should avoid cold ingredients or cold surfaces when making it, and the best way to store it is to let it dry completely and then keep it at room temperature. It is of no importance whether pasta is "fresh" or not. There is no discernible difference between pasta used immediately after it is made, while still moist, and pasta that has dried completely and been stored for several weeks. If you must buy egg pasta, look for packaged noodles that have been dried and curled into nests and check the ingredients to make sure they are made with eggs.

One of the hardest things for someone who has not grown up eating pasta in Italy is to develop the sensitivity needed to match pastas correctly with sauces. It is also one of the hardest things about pasta to try to explain. It is not a question of mere authenticity, but of attaining the best complement of flavour and texture. The same sauce can result in a mediocre dish or a fabulous dish depending on which type and shape of pasta is used. Use the recipes in this book with the pasta that is indicated or with one of the alternatives, if there are any, at the end of each recipe. This will soon train your palate to know instinctively which pasta is best suited to which sauce.

I hope this book will clear up any misconceptions about Italian pasta and provide you with the fundamental notions needed to prepare, serve and enjoy one of the greatest foods ever created. *Buon appetito!*

A CATALOGUE OF PASTA

Pasta has evolved, over its history, into an extraordinary number of varieties and shapes. The names of some shapes vary according to area, and sometimes the same name applies in different areas to different shapes. To present all the possible permutations, and every pasta from commonplace to obscure, would require an encyclopedia. This catalogue features all the pastas you are likely to encounter, arranged by shape and type.

PASTA LUNGA

Long Pasta

All pasta shapes are either long or short. The long shapes illustrated here are the dried, commercially made, flour-and-water pastas. Except for *fusilli*, these pastas are better suited to olive oil and tomato sauces than to sauces with large chunks of vegetables or meat. A good guideline is whether all the ingredients of the sauce will cling together with the long pasta when it is twirled on to a fork.

SPAGHETTI
Probably the best known of all pastas, spaghetti are a masterful invention. Their sturdy texture makes them a perfect vehicle for a wide variety of sauces.

Wholewheat, tomato and spinach spaghetti

CAPELLI D'ANGELO
The name means "angel hair", and the pasta is good with broth or, if homemade with eggs, makes a wonderful dessert (see page 148). It is never served with sauce.

SPAGHETTINI
The ini at the end of the word means small, so these are "thin spaghetti". Their delicate shape makes them ideal for light and spicy sauces.

Plain spaghetti

SAUCE SUGGESTIONS

Spaghetti are also perfect for seafood sauces, such as *frutti di mare* (page 78), prawns (page 74) or mussels (page 81). Or try *bucatini* with a tomato sauce from pages 84–5.

Spaghettini alle erbe (page 72)

Spaghetti alla carbonara (page 66)

Fusilli lunghi alla rustica (page 76)

LINGUINE

Their name means "tongues" and their flat, slippery shape is far more popular outside Italy than within it. In Italy you will find linguine only in a few areas of the south.

Bucatini

BUCATINI

Also called perciatelli, *these spaghetti-with-a-hole (like thin drinking straws) are wonderful with the robust sauces found in south-central Italy. Bucatoni are slightly fatter than bucatini.*

Bucatoni

FUSILLI LUNGHI

These are "long springs", like telephone cords. They are good with chunky sauces, which cling well to the curves in the pasta.

FETTUCCE

Ribbons

This is the most popular type of homemade egg pasta, which is at its best when rolled out by hand, resulting in a delicate, textured, porous pasta that absorbs and attracts butter- and cream-based sauces like no other. Machine-rolled egg pasta also produces a very good result, although it cannot match hand-rolled. If you must use a shop-bought egg pasta, buy only the dried version. "Fresh" egg pasta is usually of such poor quality that it is a waste of time, money and sauce.

Homemade plain and spinach pappardelle

TAGLIATELLE

Bologna is the home of tagliatelle, and the Bolognese have gone as far as to cast in gold the perfect tagliatella and display it in the Chamber of Commerce. Its most classic match is with meat Bolognese sauce (see page 62).

PAPPARDELLE

In Bologna, these are also called larghissime, which means "very wide". They are the widest ribbon and can be cut either straight or saw-edged.

Homemade plain tagliatelle, straight and in a nest

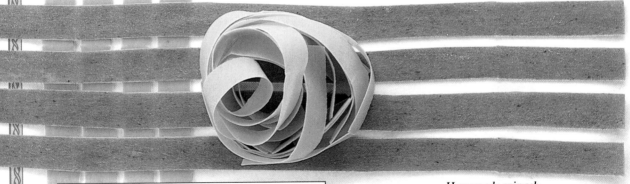

Homemade spinach tagliatelle

RIBBON PASTA WIDTHS

Approximate sizes

Tonnarelli 1.5mm (¹⁄₁₆in) square

Tagliolini 2mm (¹⁄₁₂in)

Fettuccine/trenette 5mm (¹⁄₅in)

Tagliatelle 8mm (¹⁄₃in)

Pappardelle 2cm (¾in)

PIZZOCCHERI

This pasta is made with eggs and a combination of plain and buckwheat flour. It is a speciality of the Valtellina region in Lombardy, on the Swiss border.

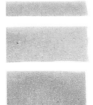

SAUCE SUGGESTIONS

For an unusual dish, try *fettuccine* with white truffles or orange and mint (page 94) or with lemon (page 96), or *tonnarelli* with melon (page 106).

Pappardelle coi fegatini di pollo (page 102)

Fettuccine all'Alfredo (page 64)

Tonnarelli al melone (page 106)

TONNARELLI

This pasta, whose shape resembles square spaghetti, *originated in Abruzzi where it is called* maccheroni alla chitarra. Chitarra *is a guitar, and the pasta was so named because it was made by pressing a thick sheet of pasta with a rolling pin through the taut wire strings of a guitar-like tool.*

Plain tonnarelli, straight and in a nest

Homemade fettuccine with nests of the shop-bought, dried version

FETTUCCINE

Also called trenette, *and probably the best known of the ribbon pastas. It is narrower than* tagliatelle *and more suited to delicate cream-based sauces.*

Spinach tagliolini

Plain tagliolini in a nest

TAGLIOLINI

This is one of the narrowest of the ribbons. It is occasionally served with a sauce but more commonly with broth.

PAGLIA E FIENO

The combination of green (spinach) and yellow (plain egg) fettuccine, cooked and served together, is called paglia e fieno, *or "straw and hay".*

17

TUBI

Tubes

Tubular pastas are sturdy, very satisfying, and go well with a variety of sauces. The cavities, especially of the larger tubes, are ideal for trapping toothsome bits in sauces. Their versatility is such that they are one of the few flour-and-water, shop-bought pastas that go well with cream sauces. There are a great many sizes of tube – some so large, such as *gigantoni*, overleaf, that you cannot toss them with a sauce and can use them only for baking.

PENNE

These are probably the most widely used of the tubular pastas. Their name means "pens", referring to their pointed, nib-shaped ends. They are available either smooth (lisce) or ridged (rigate) and in a variety of sizes. Penne ziti are fatter than regular penne. Pennoni ("fat" penne) are the largest and the least common.

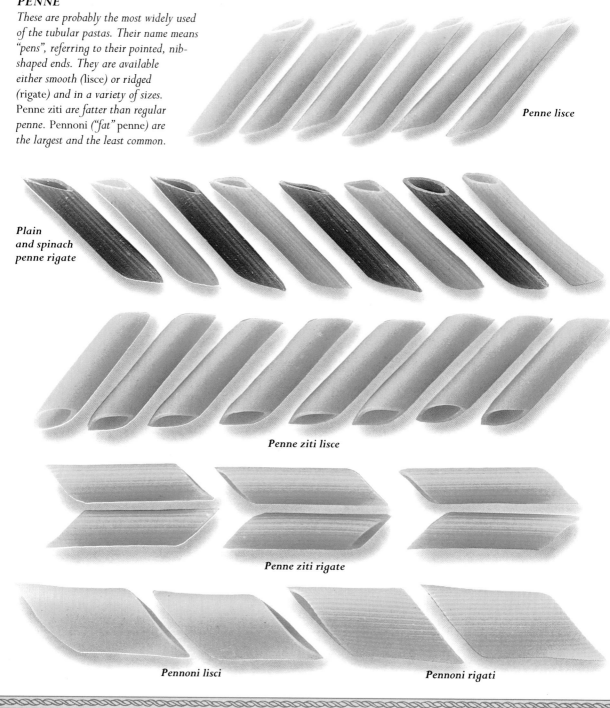

Penne lisce

Plain and spinach penne rigate

Penne ziti lisce

Penne ziti rigate

Pennoni lisci

Pennoni rigati

Small tubes are good for vegetable sauces, such as cauliflower and cream (page 108), and some meat sauces, such as chicken (page 112), or sausage (page 116).

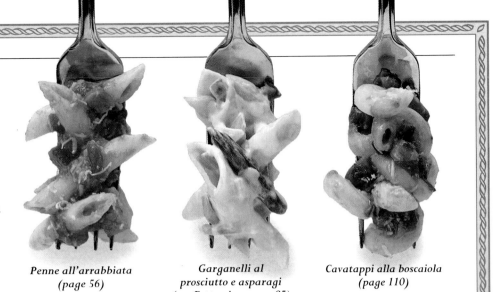

Penne all'arrabbiata
(page 56)

Garganelli al
prosciutto e asparagi
(see Fettuccine, page 95)

Cavatappi alla boscaiola
(page 110)

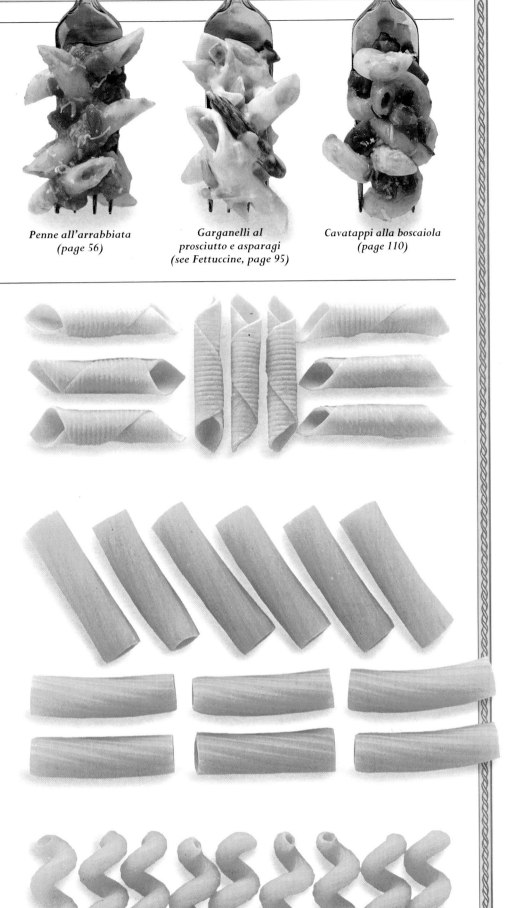

GARGANELLI

This is the only tube that is traditionally made by hand from egg pasta (see page 41 for instructions).

ELICOIDALI

The name means "helixes", and these are straight-edged tubes with ridges that curve around them. They can be used almost interchangeably with rigatoni *(see page 21), although they are narrower.*

CAVATAPPI

These are "corkscrews" and they are like an enlarged section of the long fusilli *(see page 15). They are fun to eat, their twisted shape wrapping itself wonderfully around sauces.*

TUBI
Tubes

MACCHERONI

This name was synonymous with pasta *when it first made its appearance in the aristocratic courts of southern Italy. Now* maccheroni *is a general term which can be applied to a variety of tubular pastas.* Boccolotti *and* chifferi *are mostly used in soups or with butter and cheese for small children.* Denti d'elefante, *which means "elephant's teeth", and the other two* maccheroni *shown are variations on the basic tube. The* chifferi, *below, are also called* gomiti, *or "elbow" pasta, because of their bent shape.*

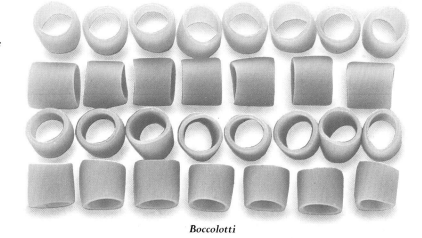

Boccolotti

Maccheroni lisci

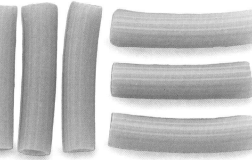

Denti d'elefante

Maccheroni rigati

Chifferi lisci

Chifferi rigati

SAUCE SUGGESTIONS

Larger tubes are ideal for meat sauces. You can also enjoy them with the *pappardelle* sauces, squab (pigeon) and chicken livers, on page 102.

Maccheroni alla salsiccia e ricotta (page 117)

Rigatoni al ragù di agnello (page 114)

Millerighe al coniglio (see Pappardelle, page 103)

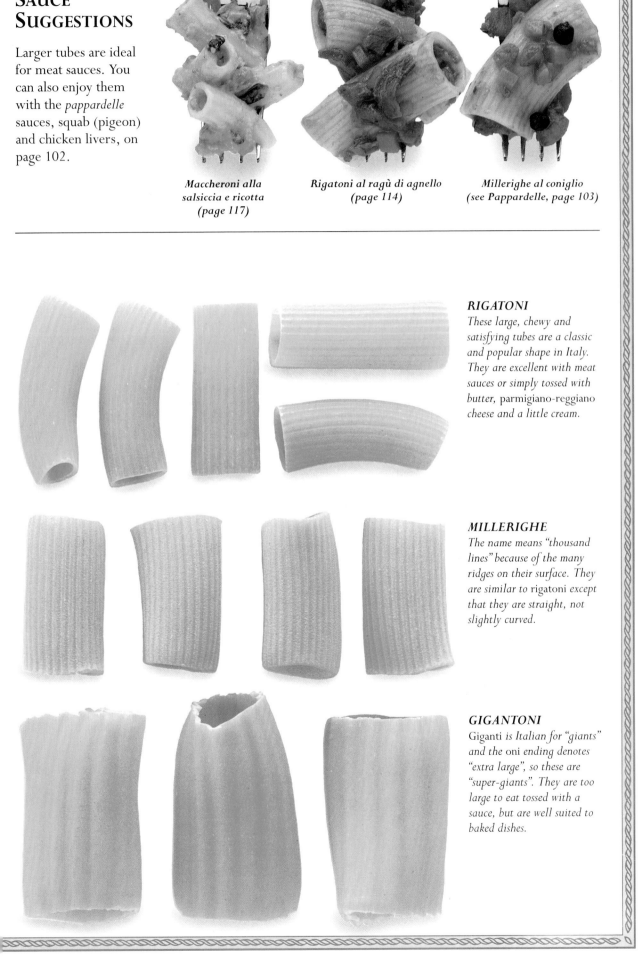

RIGATONI

These large, chewy and satisfying tubes are a classic and popular shape in Italy. They are excellent with meat sauces or simply tossed with butter, parmigiano-reggiano cheese and a little cream.

MILLERIGHE

The name means "thousand lines" because of the many ridges on their surface. They are similar to rigatoni except that they are straight, not slightly curved.

GIGANTONI

Giganti is Italian for "giants" and the oni ending denotes "extra large", so these are "super-giants". They are too large to eat tossed with a sauce, but are well suited to baked dishes.

FORME SPECIALI
Special Shapes

Italian pasta-makers have created an immense variety of special pasta shapes. New shapes are being invented all the time, but the traditional shapes tend to predominate. There is none, however, whose sole purpose is to be pleasing to the eye: each shape produces a particular sensation on the palate and is best suited to a particular type of sauce. Many of the special shapes pictured here are perfect for sauces with chunks because they can catch them in their various folds and cavities.

FARFALLE
The name means "bow-ties". Those shown here are commercially made from flour-and-water pasta, but they can be hand-made from egg pasta, as on page 41.

CONCHIGLIE
These are "shells", available in many different sizes. The smallest are usually used in soups and the middle-sized ones for sauces. The largest are generally stuffed, although they are rare in Italy because the quantity of stuffing they require overwhelms the pasta.

Beetroot, saffron and spinach tiny shells

Spinach, plain and tomato giant shells

Plain bitesize shells

Wholewheat bitesize shells

SAUCE SUGGESTIONS

You could try *lumache*, *gnocchi* or *radiatori* with artichokes, *pancetta*, lemon juice and thyme (*ai carciofi*, page 126). Or try *conchiglie*, *lumache* or *gnocchi*, each of which can hold a meaty sauce, with a *ragù* (pages 62 and 114).

Farfalle al salmone
(page 121)

Conchiglie alla
salsiccia e panna
(page 125)

Orecchiette with broccoli
(see Orecchiette alla verza,
page 129)

GNOCCHI

The real gnocchi *are potato dumplings, and these pasta shapes are made to resemble them.* Gnocchetti *are small* gnocchi, *and* sardi *indicates Sardinian style.*

Gnocchetti sardi   **Gnocchi sardi**

Riccioli (or "curly"), also known as gnocchetti

Gnocchi

LUMACHE
Their name translates as "snails", an allusion to their curled, snail-like shape. The larger one on the right is a lumacone, or "fat snail".

ORECCHIETTE
A speciality of Apulia, in southeastern Italy. The name means "little ears". They are traditionally made by hand from an eggless hardwheat pasta dough pressed between thumb and palm.

RADIATORI
These shapes are called "radiators" because they resemble little heaters.

FORME SPECIALI

Special Shapes

FUSILLI

These shapes are also referred to as fusilli corti, *or "short springs", to differentiate them from the* fusilli *shown with the long pastas (page 15).* Eliche *means propeller, and these are a slightly looser spiral. The* fusilli bucati *have a hole running through them, as indicated by the word* bucati, *which means "bored".*

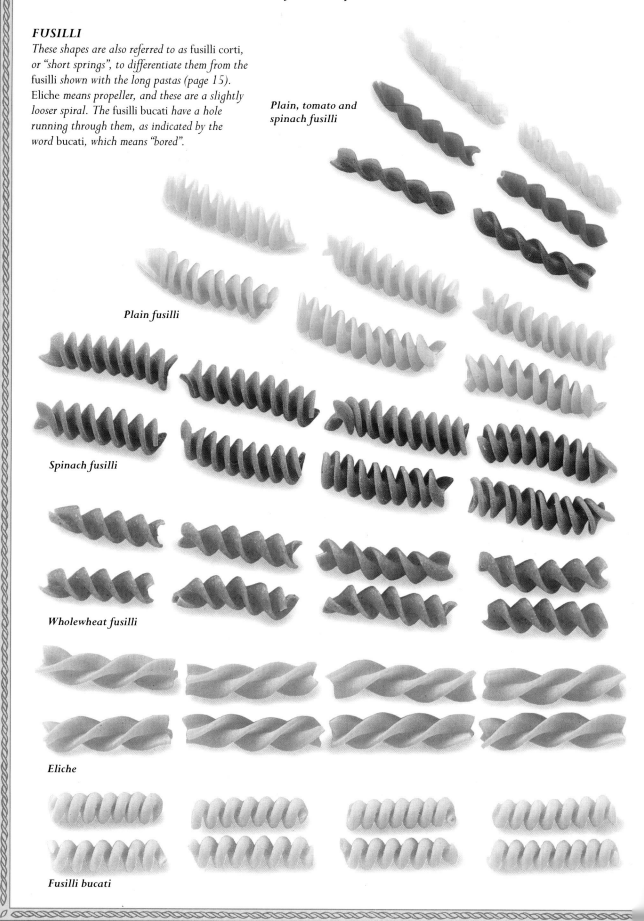

Plain, tomato and spinach fusilli

Plain fusilli

Spinach fusilli

Wholewheat fusilli

Eliche

Fusilli bucati

SAUCE SUGGESTIONS

Fusilli are versatile and therefore prominent in the pasta-lover's diet. They lend themselves well to vegetable sauces: try *alle zucchine* (shown right), *alla campagnola* (page 122), *al cavolfiore* (page 120) or *alla verza* (page 129).

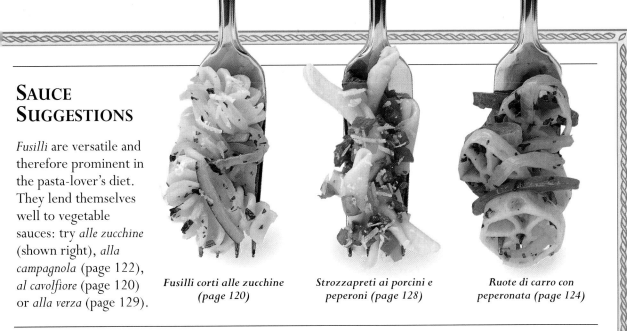

Fusilli corti alle zucchine (page 120)

Strozzapreti ai porcini e peperoni (page 128)

Ruote di carro con peperonata (page 124)

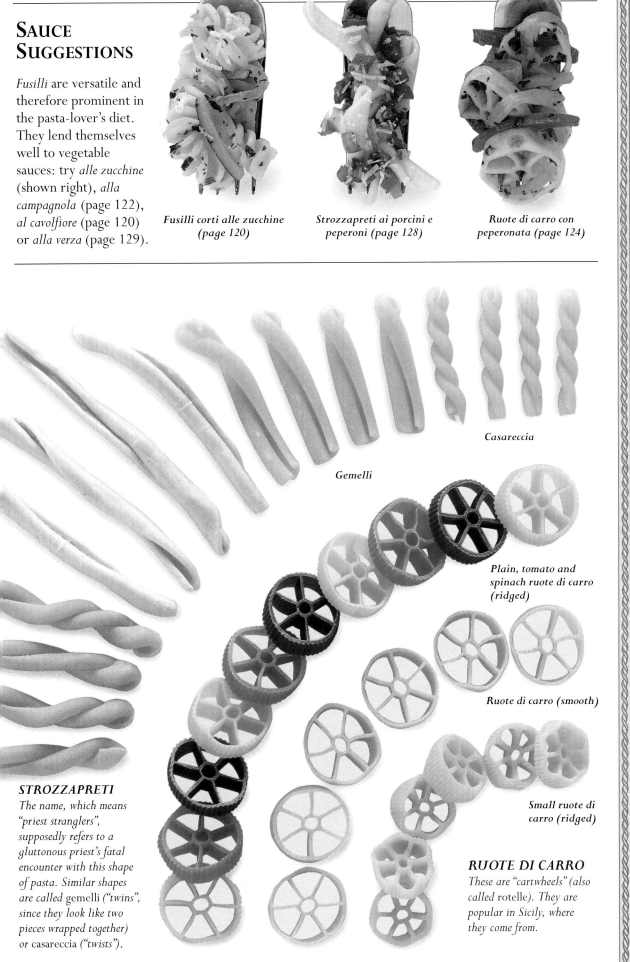

Casareccia

Gemelli

Plain, tomato and spinach ruote di carro (ridged)

Ruote di carro (smooth)

Small ruote di carro (ridged)

STROZZAPRETI

The name, which means "priest stranglers", supposedly refers to a gluttonous priest's fatal encounter with this shape of pasta. Similar shapes are called gemelli *("twins", since they look like two pieces wrapped together) or* casareccia *("twists").*

RUOTE DI CARRO

These are "cartwheels" (also called rotelle*). They are popular in Sicily, where they come from.*

PASTA PER MINESTRE
Soup Pasta

The small shapes are collectively referred to as *pastina*, "little pasta", and the endings to their names, such as *ine* or *ini* and *etti* or *ette*, indicate "small". Except for *maltagliati* and occasionally *quadrucci*, they are reserved for homemade meat broth and given as a comforting meal to children or adults feeling under the weather. The shapes that resemble rice kernels, melon seeds, peppercorns, stars and so on are created to amuse children or to look attractive rather than for differences in flavour or texture.

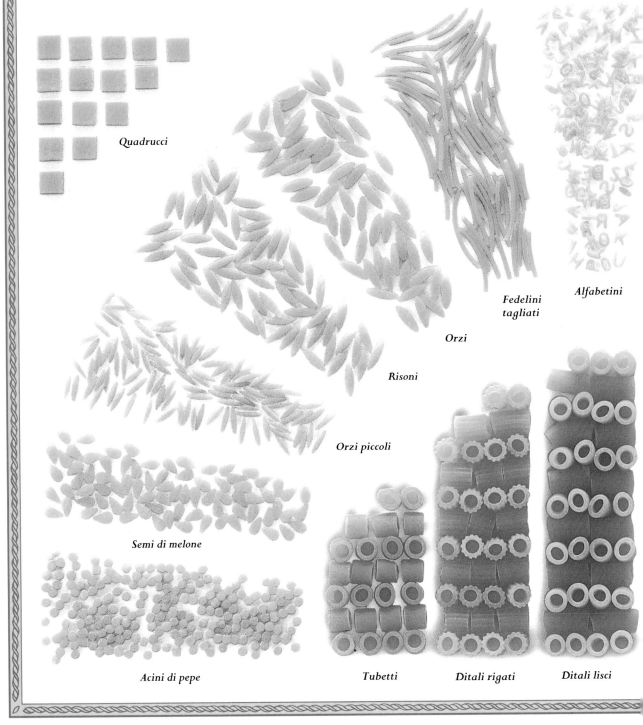

Quadrucci

Fedelini tagliati

Alfabetini

Orzi

Risoni

Orzi piccoli

Semi di melone

Acini di pepe

Tubetti

Ditali rigati

Ditali lisci

SOUP SUGGESTIONS

Maltagliati is the classic choice for pasta and bean soup (*pasta e fagioli*), far right. *Stelline*, "little stars", are used to brighten up the children's soup, centre.

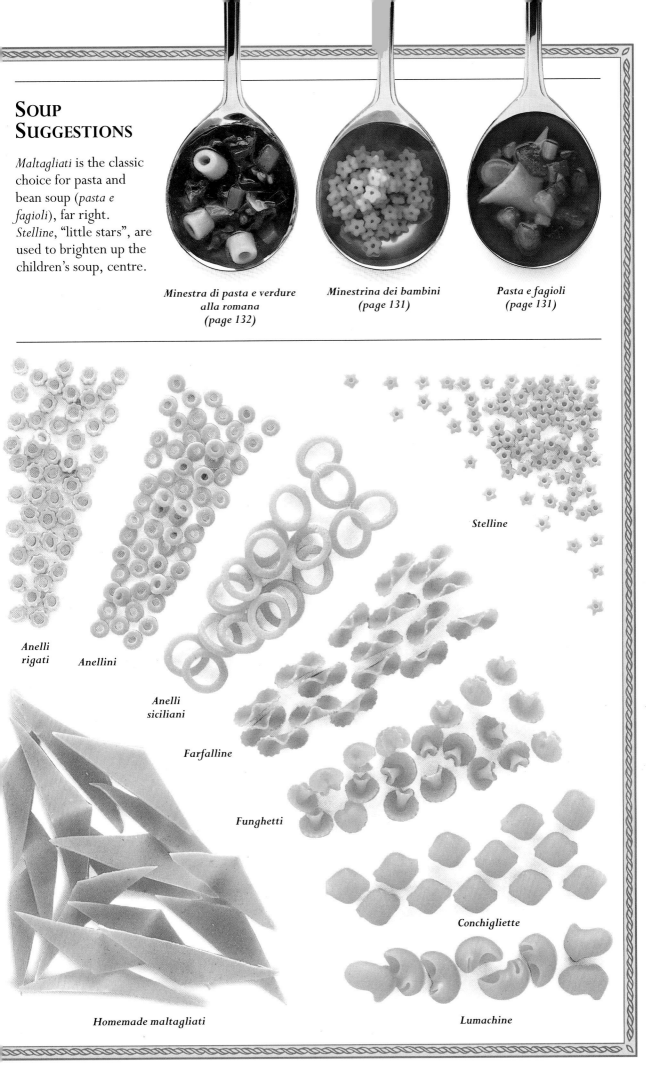

*Minestra di pasta e verdure alla romana
(page 132)*

*Minestrina dei bambini
(page 131)*

*Pasta e fagioli
(page 131)*

Stelline

Anelli rigati

Anellini

Anelli siciliani

Farfalline

Funghetti

Conchigliette

Homemade maltagliati

Lumachine

PASTA RIPIENA

Stuffed Pasta

Homemade stuffed pastas and layered pastas for baking make some of the most elegant and delicious pasta dishes. It is important that the quantity and kind of stuffing complement the shape of pasta. The most common mistake is to overpower the pasta – it should not be simply a receptacle for the stuffing but an integral part of the dish.

RAVIOLINI

Known as agnolotti *in Piedmont. They are usually filled with meat but also lend themselves to a variety of other stuffings.*

PANSOTI

Triangular pasta parcels, native to the Italian Riviera, whose name means "little bellies". They are filled with ricotta *and five local wild greens, and served with walnut* pesto *(see page 96).*

TORTELLONI

These square, stuffed pastas are usually filled with Swiss chard (or spinach) and ricotta *and served with butter and lots of* parmigiano-reggiano, *or with* Burro e pomodoro *sauce (see page 52). In Emilia they are called* tortelli.

TORTELLINI

These are a speciality of Bologna and are served with broth on New Year's Eve or else with cream sauce (see page 134).

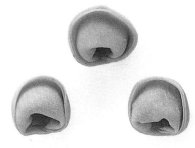

CANNELLONI

Rectangular sheets of pasta, cannelloni *are thinly spread with one of a variety of fillings, rolled up to resemble a Swiss roll and then baked.*

STUFFING SUGGESTIONS

Stuffings can be made from seafood, vegetables or meat. Cheese of some kind is usually present and egg yolk is often used to bind together the ingredients.

Sweet potato, parsley and mortadella (see Tortelli alla ferrarese, page 138)

Ricotta, minced beef and mortadella (see Cannelloni di carne, page 144)

Spinach, ricotta and prosciutto (see Tortelloni di biete, page 134)

Tortelloni

Cappelletti

CAPPELLETTI, TORTELLONI
Cappelletti are "little hats", similar to tortellini but made from a square of pasta rather than a circle so that they form a peak. The larger ones are from Bologna and are called, confusingly, tortelloni, the same name as the flat, square parcels on the opposite page.

LASAGNE
Large sheets of pasta, lasagne are used to make up the dish with which their name has become synonymous. The pasta sheets are sandwiched together with thin layers of meat, seafood or vegetable filling and then baked.

Plain and spinach lasagne

PASTA COLORATA
Coloured Pasta

Coloured and flavoured pasta is becoming increasingly popular outside Italy, but not within, where it is in conflict with the philosophy of Italian cooking whose ultimate concern is taste, rather than the appearance of food. A colour would be of no gastronomic interest unless it contributed a desirable flavour. Only spinach and tomato pastas achieve this. Outside Italy, pasta-makers are experimenting with a range of colours and flavours, as illustrated here.

PLAIN
Plain egg pasta varies from pale to rich gold in colour depending on the yolks used. Flour-and-water pasta has a warm yellow hue depending on the quality of the wheat.

TOMATO
Red pasta is traditionally made with dried tomato powder, but since this is rarely available commercially a good substitute is double-concentrate tomato purée.

SPINACH
Green pasta can be made with fresh or frozen spinach, cooked and finely chopped then added to the eggs before the flour is mixed in.

Saffron

Beetroot

Basil

Mushroom

Squid's ink

MAKING AND SERVING PASTA

Making pasta should be considered a craft, but it is one that anyone can learn and is well worth the effort. Egg pasta that is handmade from start to finish is the best. If you have a machine, use it for thinning the dough and for cutting certain widths of ribbon. Avoid machines where the ingredients are poured in at one end and a finished pasta shape is extruded from the other. They are not capable of the gradual process required to achieve the structure and texture of fine egg pasta.

PASTA-MAKING EQUIPMENT

These are all the tools you will need to make homemade egg pasta. Almost all are readily available in kitchen-supply shops or department stores. If you have difficulty finding a suitable rolling pin, try to have one custom-cut from a hardwood dowel at a timber yard. You can get by without a pasta machine if you learn to roll and cut pasta by hand.

BISCUIT CUTTERS
Straight or fluted biscuit cutters in various diameters are ideal for cutting circles of pasta for stuffing.

DOUGH SCRAPER
This is made of flexible metal or plastic and is used for scraping the sticky egg-and-flour mixture off the work surface before kneading.

SMOOTH, WARM SURFACE
Traditionally pasta dough is made on a large wooden board. A laminated plastic surface, such as formica or laminex, also works well. Cold surfaces such as marble or metal are not suitable.

FORK
Use this to beat the eggs in the flour well and to draw in the flour until the mixture is thick enough to knead.

TEA TOWEL
You need several clean and dry tea towels to absorb the moisture from freshly made pasta before it is cut, cooked or stored.

CLING FILM
When pasta dough is not being worked on, it must be wrapped tightly in cling film to prevent it from drying and forming a crust on the surface.

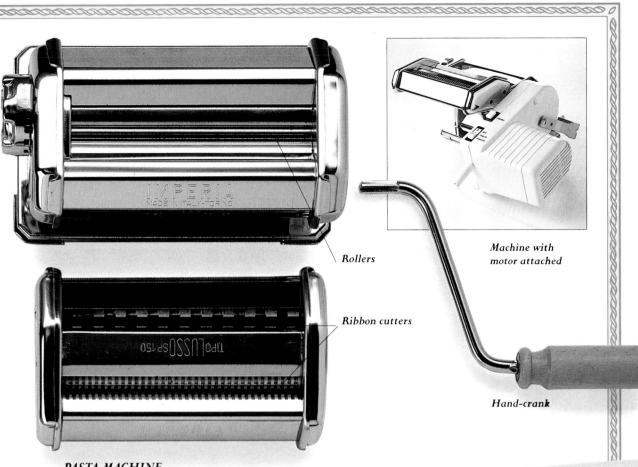

Rollers

Ribbon cutters

Machine with
motor attached

Hand-crank

PASTA MACHINE
The machine has rollers to thin out the pasta and
cutters to produce ribbons of various widths. You can
operate it with a hand-crank or an optional electric
motor. The motor is less tiring to use, frees both hands
and enables you to produce more evenly rolled sheets.

PIPING BAG
You can place fillings on a sheet of
pasta with a teaspoon, but a piping
bag will make the job easier and faster.

ROLLING PIN
The traditional pasta rolling
pin used in Bologna is 4cm
(1½in) thick and 80cm (32in)
long, with rounded, smooth
ends. However, a rolling pin up
to 5cm (2in) thick and at least
60cm (24in) long is fine for up
to three eggs' worth of dough.

PASTRY CUTTER
This rolling cutter is used for cutting
and sealing stuffed pasta and for
cutting ribbons with fluted edges.

GARGANELLI MAKER
The closest thing to an authentic Bolognese
garganelli tool is this wooden butter pat
used with a wooden dowel or round pencil
(see page 41).

KNIFE
Use a long chef's knife for cutting
pasta by hand, or the dough into
manageable chunks that can go
through the machine to be thinned.

MAKING THE DOUGH

Making pasta dough by hand is simple and with practice will easily become second nature. It also produces a far superior pasta than kneading by machine. The slower, more gradual process of hand-kneading, as well as the warmth from your hands, greatly enhances the elasticity and texture of the dough. The amount of flour given is approximate: it varies depending on the size of the eggs and the humidity of the environment. You can adjust before you begin to knead.

MIXING THE FLOUR AND EGGS

INGREDIENTS

3 size 3 eggs
300g (10oz) plain flour (for best results use Italian "OO" flour)

1 Pour the flour into a mound on a wooden or other smooth, warm work surface and make a well in the centre with your fingers.

2 Break the eggs one by one into the centre of the well.

3 Beat the eggs gently with a fork until the yolks and whites are evenly mixed together.

4 With the fork, gradually incorporate the flour from the inside of the well into the egg until the egg is no longer runny. Do not break the wall of flour or the egg will escape.

TIPS FOR MAKING THE DOUGH

• Use eggs that are at room temperature.

• Do not knead the dough on a cold surface such as marble.

COLOURED PASTA

RED PASTA

For each egg, add 1 tbsp of tomato purée. Mix it into the beaten eggs in the well before you start incorporating the flour.

GREEN PASTA

For each egg, use 125g (4oz) of fresh spinach or 75g (2½oz) of thawed frozen spinach. Cook in salted water (this enhances the colour), squeeze out excess water and finely chop before using.

KNEADING THE DOUGH

1 This step must be done quickly and without hesitation or you may end up losing some of the egg mixture. Using both hands, swiftly bring the remaining flour over the egg mixture so that it is completely covered.

2 Begin working the mass with your hands until all the flour is mixed in with the eggs. Decide whether you need more flour: the dough should feel moist but not sticky. When it is the right consistency, wrap it tightly in cling film.

3 Scrape away any dough stuck to the work surface, and wash your hands to remove any egg and flour. Unwrap the dough and begin kneading. Hold the dough with one hand while folding it over with the fingers of the other hand.

4 Use the heel of your palm to push the dough down and away from you. Rotate the dough a quarter turn and repeat the two-part process. Continue until the dough is uniform and very smooth. Immediately wrap it in cling film and leave it to rest for at least 20 minutes before rolling it out.

ROLLING THE PASTA

Rolling by hand produces a more desirable pasta than rolling by machine. When you roll by hand the dough is stretched rather than compressed. This creates a more porous pasta which absorbs sauce better as well as having a more interesting texture. Practise a couple of times on dough that you are happy to discard until you feel you have got it right. If you do use a machine, get the optional motor attachment so that your hands are free to feed in the dough.

ROLLING BY HAND

Be prepared to throw away your first few hand-rolled sheets – you are unlikely to get the hang of rolling pasta in one go. First remove the dough from the cling film. Knead it again for about a minute so that the moisture that has collected on the surface is worked back into the dough. Flatten the dough a little with your hands to form a round disc and place it on the work surface.

1 *Begin rolling from two-thirds of the way down the disc until just before the top edge. Stop, turn the disc 90°, and repeat. Continue until the dough is 6mm (¼in) thick.*

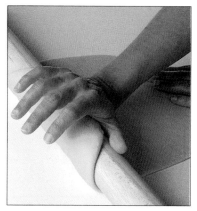

2 *Roll the top edge of the dough on to the pin. Hold the dough at the bottom while you gently stretch and roll it on to the pin. Turn the dough on the pin 90°, unroll and repeat five times.*

3 *Roll the dough snugly back on to the pin from the top. As you roll the pin back and forth, slide your hands together and apart to trace the shape of a W. When the dough is rolled up, turn it with the pin, unroll and repeat.*

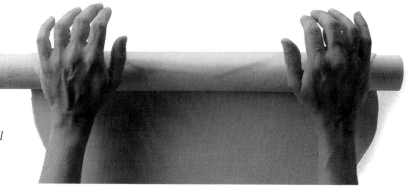

4 *Continue stretching the dough until it is transparent, letting it drape over the edge of the worktop. Cut it if it gets too big. Leave on a tea towel to dry.*

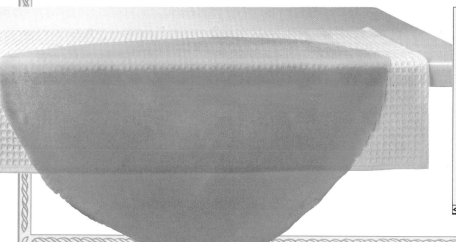

TIPS FOR HAND-ROLLING

• *Have only the palms of your hands in contact with the dough on the rolling pin.*

• *To stretch rather than compress the dough, do not push down on it but out and away from you.*

ROLLING BY MACHINE

Thin the dough through the machine one notch at a time. Trying to speed the thinning process by skipping notches on the rollers will result in pasta of a poor texture. Pasta needs to be thinned out gradually to give it elasticity.

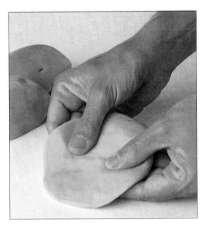

1 Cut a three-egg dough into at least six pieces. Flatten one with your fingers and wrap the rest in cling film.

TIPS FOR ROLLING BY MACHINE

• *You need a lot of worktop space for all the rolled-out dough so do, say, three pieces at a time, and keep the rest in cling film.*

• *Cut the strip if, as it thins, it becomes too long and unwieldy.*

2 With the rollers at their widest setting, feed the dough into the machine. Pick up the dough as it comes through but don't stretch or pull it.

3 Fold the dough in three, turn it so the folds are at the sides, and run it through the machine again. Do this three or four times until the dough is very smooth. Repeat with the other pieces.

4 Reduce the width of the rollers by one notch. Run all the pieces through the machine once, laying them out on dry tea towels. Reduce the width by one notch again, and repeat. Continue until all the pieces have gone through the machine at each setting down to the thinnest.

CUTTING THE PASTA

Before you cut pasta it must dry until it feels leathery so that the noodles will not stick to each other, but not dry so much that it becomes too brittle to cut. If you use a pasta machine to roll out the dough, the pieces will be just the right size and shape to feed back through the machine's cutting attachment to make *fettuccine* and *tonnarelli*. Other shapes need to be cut by hand, which is simple and requires only a little practice. Hand-rolled pasta must, of course, be hand-cut.

CUTTING BY HAND

FETTUCCINE (5mm / ⅕in) AND TAGLIATELLE (8mm / ⅓in)

1 Loosely roll up the sheet of pasta dough into a flat roll about 5cm (2in) across.

2 Take a large knife, rest the flat of the blade against your knuckles and cut the roll of pasta into ribbons of the desired width by moving your knuckles back along the roll after every cut.

3 Unravel the ribbons. To store them (dried pasta keeps for months), wrap loosely round your hand into nests and put on a tea towel to dry. To use the same day, lay them flat on a towel.

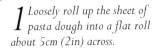

CAPELLI D'ANGELO
To make angel hair, follow the procedure above but cut the pasta as thinly as possible.

MALTAGLIATI
Make two diagonal cuts followed by a straight cut perpendicular to the roll of pasta. Separate the little piles.

QUADRUCCI
Cut the pasta as for tagliatelle, above, then, without unravelling, cut the ribbons crossways into small squares.

PAPPARDELLE

To make the saw-edged version, use a fluted pastry cutter on flat sheets of pasta. For straight-edged, roll up the pasta and cut ribbons 2cm (¾in) wide.

FARFALLE

Cut a sheet of pasta into 4cm (1½in) squares using a fluted pastry cutter. Pinch the squares in the middle, with one fold on top and two on the bottom.

GARGANELLI

Roll 4cm (1½in) pasta squares on to a pencil over the teeth of a comb or butter pat. Press down on the pencil edges, not the pasta itself, and the garganelli will slide off easily.

CUTTING BY MACHINE

FETTUCCINE

Roll the pasta to the thinnest setting of the rollers. Use a knife to cut the pasta into strips around 30cm (12in) long. Attach the cutters to the machine and pass the strips of pasta through the wider set. Store machine-cut pasta in the same way as hand-cut pasta.

TONNARELLI

Thin the pasta to the penultimate setting of the rollers, then pass the sheets through the narrower cutters of the machine attachment. Because the pasta sheet is thick, and the cutting measure narrow, the resulting ribbon is square in cross-section.

STUFFING THE PASTA

Except for *tortellini* and *cappelletti*, which require a little bit of practice, all the other stuffed pasta shapes are easy to make and require no special skill. Your biggest enemy in making stuffed pastas will be pasta that is too dry to work with.

To help avoid that problem, always keep the dough you are not working on tightly wrapped in cling film until you are ready to use it. You could also add about 10ml (2 teaspoons) of milk to a two-egg batch of dough when you mix in the eggs.

TORTELLONI

1 Tortelloni in Romagna, tortelli in Emilia are squares of pasta with filling in the middle. Take a strip of pasta 10cm (4in) wide and place stuffing on it at 5cm (2in) intervals. You need the equivalent of a rounded teaspoon of stuffing.

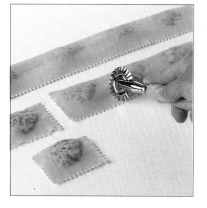

2 Moisten the edges of the pasta and fold it over. Cut between the stuffing (at 5cm/2in intervals) and along the bottom edge with a fluted cutter. Pinch the edges together to seal.

TORTELLINI

2 Fold the disc in half then pull the two corners together, wrapping them around the tip of your finger. Pinch them together where they join.

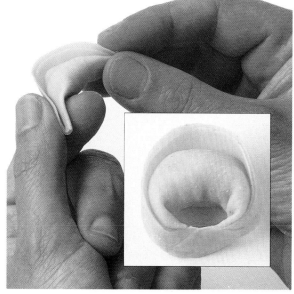

1 Cut 5cm (2in) discs from a thin sheet of pasta using a plain biscuit cutter. Place about ½ teaspoon of stuffing in the centre of each disc.

TORTELLONI FROM BOLOGNA

1 For Bolognese tortelloni, *cut a thin sheet of pasta into 7.5cm (3in) squares and place about a rounded teaspoon of stuffing in the centre of each one.*

2 *Moisten the edges with a wet finger and fold each square in half to form a triangle. Pinch the edges together to seal.*

3 *Pull two corners together, wrapping them around the tip of your finger and indenting the parcel where filled with stuffing. Pinch the corners together where they join.*

RAVIOLINI

1 Cut 5cm (2in) discs from a thin *sheet of pasta using a fluted biscuit cutter.*

2 *Place about ½ teaspoon of stuffing in the centre of each disc.*

3 *Fold each disc in half, pinching the edges with your fingers to seal them. Gently pull down the two corners to form a crescent.*

VARIATIONS

PANSOTI
Place stuffing in the centre of 5cm (2in) squares of pasta and fold in half.

RAVIOLINI
For smooth-edged raviolini, *use a plain biscuit cutter or a glass.*

CAPPELLETTI
These are like tortellini *but made from a square. They resemble bishop's mitres.*

COOKING AND SERVING

Cooking pasta is simple and only requires a little practice and intuition. Ignore the directions on dried, shop-bought pasta: the only way of knowing when it is done is to taste it. It should be firm to the bite but chewable. Remember, it will continue to cook as you drain and toss it. Cooking time will vary with the shape and brand. Homemade pasta cooks very quickly. If newly made, it cooks in less than a minute. For stuffed pastas, taste the edge where the parcel is sealed.

BOILING THE PASTA

1 Use a large saucepan or pot so that there is room for the pasta to move around in the water. Bring the water to the boil before adding salt or pasta. Add all the pasta at once.

2 Stir the pasta straight away to prevent it from sticking to the pot or to itself, and also to submerge long strands. Never break long pasta to fit it into the pot. Cover the pot until the water resumes boiling.

3 Stir periodically and taste to see if the pasta is al dente, or firm to the bite. At this point, it is done.

4 Drain the pasta through a colander immediately. Shake to dislodge excess water. Never rinse the pasta – this chills it, as well as removing its coat of starch which helps it to cling to the sauce.

PASTA-TO-WATER

½ packet (250g) pasta
3 litres (5 pints) water

1 packet (500g) pasta
4 litres (7 pints) water

1½ packets (750g) pasta
5 litres (9 pints) water

2 packets (1kg) pasta
Use two pots

SALT

1 tbsp salt for
4 litres (7 pints) water

SERVING

1 Transfer the pasta to a
warmed serving bowl and
add the sauce. Alternatively,
add the pasta to the pan
containing the sauce.

2 Toss with a fork and a spoon
until the pasta is thoroughly
coated with the sauce. Avoid
the common mistake of
serving a heap of pasta
with the sauce simply
placed on top of it.

TWIRLING

To twirl long pasta on to a fork, pick up
a few strands, lifting them away from
the others. With the tip of the fork
prongs against the side of the plate,
rotate the fork until the strands are
completely rolled on to it. The
knack is to pick up only a few
strands at the outset or you will
end up with an unmanageable
ball of pasta on your fork.

CLASSIC SAUCES

The pasta sauces here are some of the more popular traditional ones. A definitive recipe does not exist for any of them; instead there are many versions, all of which are equally authentic. Mine are based on personal preference, and on the way I have eaten them and seen them being made as I was growing up.

Each recipe serves 6 people if followed by a second course, or 4 people if served on its own

SPAGHETTINI
AGLIO E OLIO

Spaghettini with Garlic and Olive Oil

This dish has been my saviour during many a late-night hunger attack. It is quick and easy and, with good quality pasta and olive oil, immensely satisfying. Take the sauce off the heat as soon as it is ready, even if the pasta is not yet done. The oil will hold its heat for the extra minutes you need to finish off the pasta, and you will avoid the risk of burning the garlic.

Extra-virgin olive oil

INGREDIENTS

For 500g (1lb) dried, shop-bought pasta

120ml (8 tbsps) extra-virgin olive oil
1 tsp finely chopped garlic
1 tbsp finely chopped flat-leaf parsley
¼ tsp crushed chillies
salt

PREPARATION

1 Bring 4 litres (7 pints) of water to the boil in a large saucepan or pot, add 1 tablespoon of salt and drop in the pasta all at once, stirring until the strands are submerged.
2 Put the olive oil and garlic in a large sauté pan over a medium-high heat. When the garlic begins to change colour, add the parsley, crushed chillies and some salt. Stir well and remove from the heat.
3 When the pasta is cooked *al dente*, return the pan with the sauce to a low heat, drain the pasta and add it to the pan. Toss until the pasta is well coated with the sauce, taste for salt and spiciness, and serve at once.

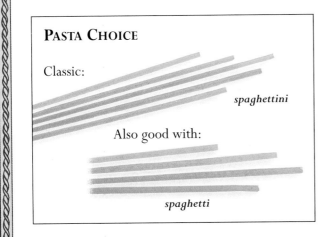

PASTA CHOICE

Classic:

spaghettini

Also good with:

spaghetti

Garlic

Flat-leaf parsley

Crushed
chillies

Salt

**Spaghettini
aglio e olio**

PESTO DI BASILICO
ALLA GENOVESE
Genoese Basil Pesto

The only way to have true Genoese *pesto* is to go to the Liguria region of Italy where the tiny fragrant sweet basil for which the Italian Riviera is famous can be found. Locally grown basil, although not quite the same, will produce a perfectly acceptable alternative for those of us who may find it impractical to fly to the Riviera whenever we feel like having *pesto*.

INGREDIENTS

For pasta made with 3 eggs (see page 36)
or **500g (1lb) dried, shop-bought pasta**

60g (2oz) fresh basil leaves
120ml (8 tbsps) extra-virgin olive oil
2 tbsps pine nuts
2 cloves garlic, peeled
salt
60g (2oz) freshly grated parmigiano-reggiano *cheese*
2 tbsps freshly grated pecorino romano *cheese*
45g (1½oz) butter, softened to room temperature

PREPARATION

1 Put the basil leaves, olive oil, pine nuts, garlic and 1 teaspoon of salt into a food processor or blender and grind until fine and almost creamy.

You can prepare the sauce ahead of time up to this point and refrigerate or even freeze it. Cover the surface with olive oil to prevent the basil from oxidizing and turning black.

2 Transfer the mixture to a large bowl and stir in the two grated cheeses.
3 Drop the pasta into 4 litres (7 pints) of boiling water with 1 tablespoon of salt, stir well and cook until *al dente*. Drain and toss with the sauce, 2 tablespoons of hot water and the butter.

Extra-virgin olive oil

Basil

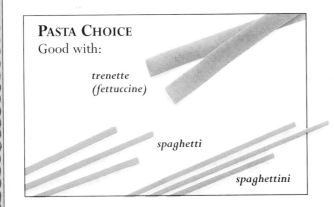

PASTA CHOICE
Good with:

trenette (fettuccine)

spaghetti

spaghettini

Pine nuts

Garlic

Salt

Parmigiano-reggiano

Pecorino romano

Butter

**Trenette with
pesto di basilico**

SUGO AL
BURRO E POMODORO
Butter and Tomato Sauce

This is probably the simplest of all pasta sauces and will evoke childhood memories for many an Italian. If you want a pure tomato sauce, it has no equal. Use fresh tomatoes if you can, although tinned are better than poor-quality fresh ones.

INGREDIENTS

For pasta made with 3 eggs (see page 36)
or 500g (1lb) dried, shop-bought pasta

*1kg (2lb) fresh ripe plum tomatoes, peeled, seeded and coarsely chopped, **or** 2 x 400g (14oz) tins whole peeled tomatoes, with their juice, coarsely chopped*
100g (3½oz) butter
1 medium-sized onion, peeled and cut in half
salt
4 tbsps freshly grated parmigiano-reggiano cheese

PREPARATION

1 Put all the ingredients except the cheese in a saucepan and simmer over a low heat until the tomatoes have reduced and separated from the butter: 20–40 minutes depending on the size of the pan. Remove from the heat and set aside, discarding the onion halves.

You can prepare the sauce ahead of time and refrigerate (it keeps for 3–4 days in the refrigerator in a tightly lidded jar) or freeze it.

2 Drop the pasta into 4 litres (7 pints) of boiling water with 1 tablespoon of salt, stir well and cook until *al dente*. Drain and toss with the hot or reheated sauce and the freshly grated cheese.

Fresh plum tomatoes

Butter

Onion

PEELING A TOMATO

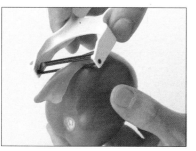

1 *Peel the tomato using a swivel-bladed peeler. Use a side-to-side, sawing motion at the same time as you peel downwards.*

2 *Halve the tomato then scoop out the seeds with your thumb and discard them. You can then coarsely chop the tomato flesh.*

**Tortelloni di spinaci
with sugo al burro
e pomodoro**

Salt

Parmigiano-reggiano

PASTA CHOICE
Good with:

bucatini

penne lisce

*tortelloni
di spinaci*

spaghetti

SPAGHETTINI AL
POMODORO E BASILICO

Spaghettini with Tomatoes, Basil, Olive Oil and Garlic

This is a quick and easy summery sauce, one I can eat often without tiring of it, and ideal when fresh, ripe tomatoes are abundant. The crushed chillies, if you choose to use them, are not intended to make the sauce spicy but simply to give it a little liveliness, so be gentle with the pinch, and while the amount of garlic may seem overgenerous, it is less pungent when sliced and stewed than when chopped and browned. You get a sweeter flavour from fresh tomatoes than from tinned.

INGREDIENTS

For 500g (1lb) dried, shop-bought pasta

75ml (5 tbsps) extra-virgin olive oil
3 tbsps thinly sliced garlic
1kg (2lb) fresh ripe plum tomatoes, peeled, seeded and thinly sliced lengthways, or 2 x 400g (14oz) tins whole peeled tomatoes, with their juice, coarsely chopped
salt
4 tbsps fresh basil leaves, torn by hand into 1cm (½in) pieces
pinch of crushed chillies (optional)

PREPARATION

1 Put all but 1 tablespoon of the olive oil and all the garlic in a large sauté pan over a medium-high heat and cook until the garlic begins to sizzle.
2 Add the tomatoes as soon as you see the garlic begin to change colour. If using fresh, you'll notice they give off a fair amount of liquid. When the liquid begins to reduce, season with salt. If using tinned, season with salt straightaway. Continue cooking over a medium-high heat until the tomatoes have reduced and separated from the oil: 10–20 minutes depending on the size of the pan.
3 While the sauce is reducing, pour 4 litres (7 pints) of water into a large saucepan or pot and place over a high heat.
4 When the sauce has reduced, add the torn basil leaves and the optional pinch of crushed chillies. Cook for 1–2 minutes, then remove from the heat and set aside.
5 When the water for the pasta is boiling, add 1 tablespoon of salt and drop in the pasta all at once, stirring until the strands are submerged. When cooked *al dente*, drain and toss with the sauce in the pan, adding the remaining tablespoon of olive oil. Taste for salt and serve at once.

Garlic

Extra-virgin olive oil

PASTA CHOICE
Classic:

spaghettini

Also good with:

spaghetti

penne lisce

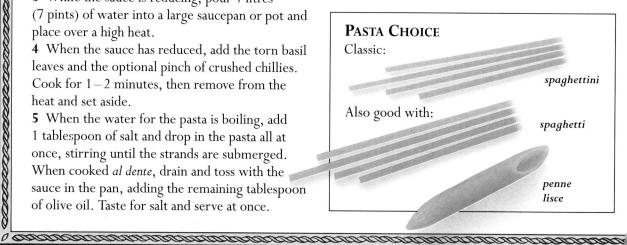

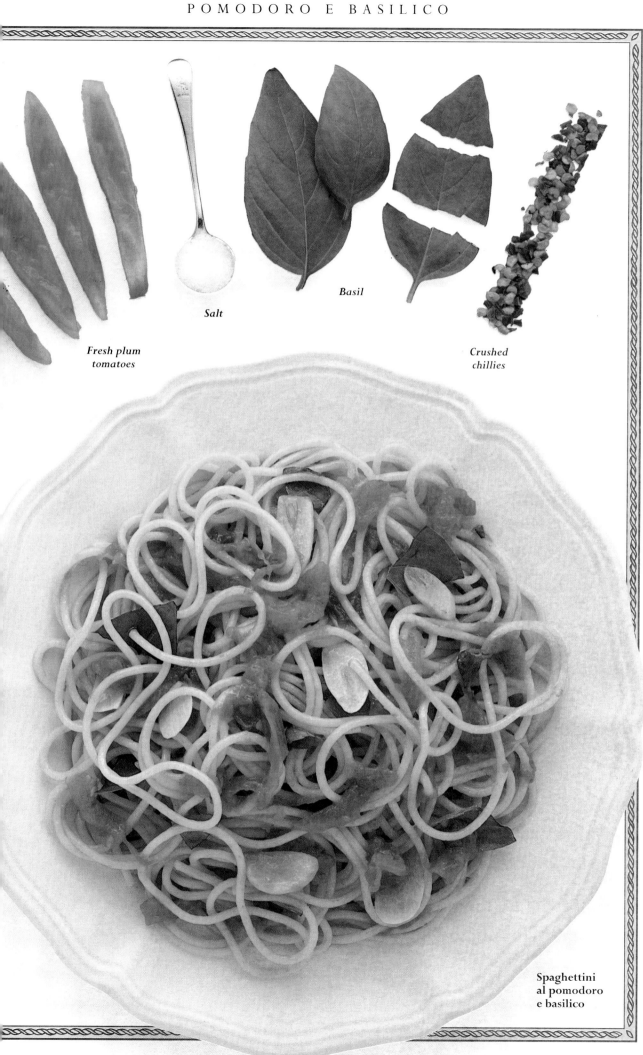

Fresh plum
tomatoes

Salt

Basil

Crushed
chillies

Spaghettini
al pomodoro
e basilico

PENNE
ALL'ARRABBIATA

Penne with Spicy Tomato Sauce

This is, literally, an "angry" pasta, which means it is hot and spicy, and it is popular in Rome and central Italy. Increase or decrease the amount of crushed chillies according to the intensity of "anger" you desire.

INGREDIENTS

For 500g (1lb) dried, shop-bought pasta

100ml (7 tbsps) extra-virgin olive oil
½ tsp finely chopped garlic
60g (2oz) pancetta, cut from a 6mm (¼in) thick slice into thin strips
2 x 400g (14oz) tins whole peeled tomatoes, with their juice, coarsely chopped
¼ tsp crushed chillies
salt
12 medium-sized fresh basil leaves, torn by hand into 1cm (½in) pieces
2 tbsps freshly grated pecorino romano cheese

PASTA CHOICE
Classic:

penne rigate

Also good with:

spaghetti

Extra-virgin olive oil

Garlic

Pancetta

PREPARATION

1 Put all but 1 tablespoon of the olive oil and all the garlic in a large sauté pan over a medium-high heat and cook until the garlic begins to sizzle.
2 Add the *pancetta* strips and cook until the *pancetta* is well browned but not crisp.
3 Add the tinned tomatoes, the crushed chillies and a little salt (remembering that the *pancetta* is already salty). Reduce the heat and simmer until the tomatoes have reduced and separated from the oil: 30–40 minutes depending on the size of the pan. Remove from the heat and set aside.

You can prepare the sauce ahead of time up to this point and refrigerate it.

4 Bring 4 litres (7 pints) of water to the boil in a large saucepan or pot, add 1 tablespoon of salt and drop in the pasta all at once, stirring well.
5 Return the pan with the sauce to a medium heat and add the torn basil leaves. When the pasta is cooked *al dente*, drain and toss with the sauce in the pan, turning off the heat. Stir in the remaining tablespoon of olive oil and the grated cheese. Taste for salt and spiciness and serve at once.

Penne
all'arrabbiata

Pecorino
romano

Tinned
tomatoes

Crushed
chillies

Salt

Basil

SPAGHETTI ALLA
PUTTANESCA

Spaghetti with Tomatoes, Capers, Olives and Anchovies

Puttana means whore and this is the pasta dish she would use to seduce her clients. While I cannot guarantee its success as an aphrodisiac, I can at least guarantee that your partner will enjoy the food!

Extra-virgin olive oil

Anchovies

Garlic

Tinned tomatoes

INGREDIENTS

For 500g (1lb) dried, shop-bought pasta

100ml (7 tbsps) extra-virgin olive oil
6 anchovy fillets, chopped
½ tsp finely chopped garlic
2 x 400g (14oz) tins whole peeled tomatoes,
with their juice, coarsely chopped
salt
2 tsps coarsely chopped fresh oregano or ½ tsp dried
2 tbsps capers
8 – 10 black olives, flesh sliced from around stone

PREPARATION

1 Put all but 1 tablespoon of the olive oil and all the anchovies in a large sauté pan over a low heat and cook, stirring with a wooden spoon, until the anchovies dissolve.

2 Add the garlic and cook for about 15 seconds, taking care not to brown it.

3 Raise the heat to medium-high and add the tomatoes with a tiny pinch of salt. When the sauce comes to the boil, turn the heat down and simmer until the tomatoes have reduced and separated from the oil: 20–40 minutes depending on the size of the pan. Remove from the heat and set aside.

You can prepare the sauce ahead of time up to this point and refrigerate it.

4 Bring 4 litres (7 pints) of water to the boil in a large saucepan or pot, add 1 tablespoon of salt and drop in the pasta all at once, stirring until the strands are submerged.

5 When the pasta is halfway done, return the pan with the sauce to a medium heat, adding the oregano, capers and olives.

6 When the pasta is cooked *al dente*, drain and toss with the sauce in the pan over a low heat, adding the remaining tablespoon of olive oil. Taste for salt and serve at once.

**Spaghetti alla
puttanesca**

Salt

Fresh oregano

Capers

Olives

PASTA CHOICE

Classic: Also good with:

spaghettini

spaghetti *penne lisce*

FETTUCCINE
PRIMAVERA

Fettuccine with Spring Vegetables and Cream

Outside Italy this recipe is as popular to eat as it is common to mis-cook. The most frequent mistake is to fail to sauté the vegetables for long enough to concentrate their flavour. Done properly, this is a perfectly balanced, heavenly dish.

Carrots

INGREDIENTS

For pasta made with 3 eggs (see page 36)
or 500g (1lb) dried, shop-bought pasta

125g (4oz) asparagus
60g (2oz) butter
4 tbsps finely chopped onion
4 tbsps finely chopped celery
60g (2oz) finely diced carrots
60g (2oz) finely diced courgettes
4 tbsps peeled and finely diced red pepper
salt and freshly ground black pepper
250ml (8fl oz) double cream
30g (1oz) freshly grated parmigiano-reggiano *cheese*
2 tbsps finely chopped flat-leaf parsley

Celery

PREPARATION

1 Trim and peel the lower green portions of the asparagus. Cook whole in salted boiling water in a sauté pan until tender. Cut into 1cm (½in) lengths.
2 Melt the butter in a large sauté pan over a medium-high heat. Put in the onion and sauté to a rich golden colour. Add the celery and carrot and sauté for another 5 minutes.
3 Add the courgette and red pepper and continue to sauté over a medium-high heat until all the vegetables are tender and lightly coloured (approximately 10–20 minutes, depending on the size of the pan). Add salt and black pepper to taste.
4 Put the asparagus in with the vegetables and sauté for about a minute. Add the cream and cook, stirring occasionally, until the cream has reduced by half, then remove from the heat and set aside.
5 While the cream is reducing, pour 4 litres (7 pints) of water into a large saucepan or pot and place over a high heat. When the water is boiling, and the sauce is off the heat, add 1 tablespoon of salt to the water and drop in the pasta, stirring.
6 When the pasta is cooked *al dente*, return the pan with the sauce to a medium heat, drain the pasta and toss it with the sauce, adding the grated cheese and the parsley. Serve at once.

Onion

Butter

Asparagus

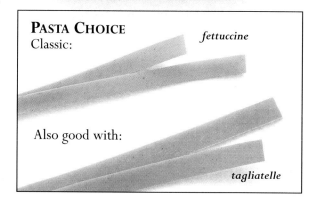

PASTA CHOICE
Classic: *fettuccine*

Also good with:

tagliatelle

Courgettes

Red pepper

Salt

Black
pepper

Double cream

Parmigiano-
reggiano

Flat-leaf parsley

**Fettuccine
primavera**

TAGLIATELLE AL
RAGU

Tagliatelle with Meat Bolognese Sauce

As a child, my mouth would water in anticipation of those glorious moments when we would sit at the table and a steaming platter of *tagliatelle al ragù* with its irresistible aroma would arrive. The dish is a staple in Emilia-Romagna, the region where my family comes from, and is almost synonymous with its capital city, Bologna. This is the way my mother makes it, and the way my grandmother made it …

Onion

INGREDIENTS

For pasta made with 3 eggs (see page 36)
or **500g (1lb) dried, shop-bought pasta**

45ml (3 tbsps) extra-virgin olive oil
75g (2½oz) butter
2 tbsps finely chopped onion
2 tbsps finely diced carrot
2 tbsps finely diced celery
350g (12oz) coarsely minced lean beef
salt
250ml (8fl oz) dry white wine
120ml (8 tbsps) full-cream milk
⅛ tsp freshly grated nutmeg
500g (1lb) tinned whole peeled tomatoes,
with their juice, coarsely chopped
60g (2oz) freshly grated parmigiano-reggiano *cheese*

Butter

Extra-virgin olive oil

PREPARATION

1 Put the olive oil, just over half of the butter and all the onion in a heavy-bottomed, deep saucepan over a medium-high heat and sauté until the onion has turned a light golden colour.
2 Add the carrot and celery and continue sautéing until they begin to change colour.
3 Put in the beef, breaking it up with a wooden spoon. Sprinkle on a little salt and cook, stirring occasionally, until the meat has lost its raw colour.
4 Pour in the wine and cook, stirring occasionally, until it has completely evaporated. Pour in the milk, sprinkle on the nutmeg and continue to cook, stirring, until most of the milk has evaporated.
5 Add the tomatoes, stir, and once they start to bubble, turn the heat down to very low. Simmer uncovered for at least 3 hours, stirring occasionally.

You can prepare the sauce ahead of time up to this point and refrigerate or even freeze it. When reheating it, add a couple of tablespoons of water.

6 Drop the pasta into 4 litres (7 pints) of boiling water with 1 tablespoon of salt, stir well and cook until *al dente*. Drain and toss with the hot or reheated sauce, the remaining butter and the freshly grated cheese. Taste for salt and serve at once.

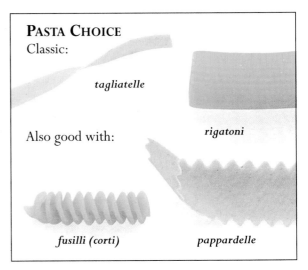

PASTA CHOICE
Classic:

tagliatelle

rigatoni

Also good with:

fusilli (corti)

pappardelle

Carrot

Celery

Minced
beef

Salt

White wine

Milk

Nutmeg

Tinned
tomatoes

Parmigiano-
reggiano

**Tagliatelle
al ragù**

FETTUCCINE
ALL'ALFREDO

Fettuccine with Butter and Cream

This is commonly thought of as a northern Italian dish but it actually comes from Rome. It is named after a restaurant owner, Alfredo, whose trademark was to give his pasta a final toss with a gold fork and spoon before sending it to the table.

INGREDIENTS

For pasta made with 3 eggs (see page 36)
or **500g (1lb) dried, shop-bought pasta**

45g (1½oz) butter
250ml (8fl oz) double cream
pinch of freshly ground nutmeg
salt and freshly ground black pepper
60g (2oz) freshly grated parmigiano-reggiano *cheese*

PREPARATION

1 Pour 4 litres (7 pints) of water into a large saucepan or pot and place over a high heat.
2 Put the butter and cream in a large sauté pan over a medium-high heat and boil, stirring frequently, until the cream has reduced almost by half. Add the freshly grated nutmeg, some salt and a generous grinding of the pepper mill. Remove from the heat and set aside.
3 When the water for the pasta is boiling, and the sauce is off the heat, add 1 tablespoon of salt to the boiling water and drop in the pasta all at once, stirring well. When the pasta is cooked *al dente*, drain it and add it to the sauce in the pan.
4 Add the grated cheese, toss until the pasta is well coated with the sauce, taste for salt and pepper and serve at once.

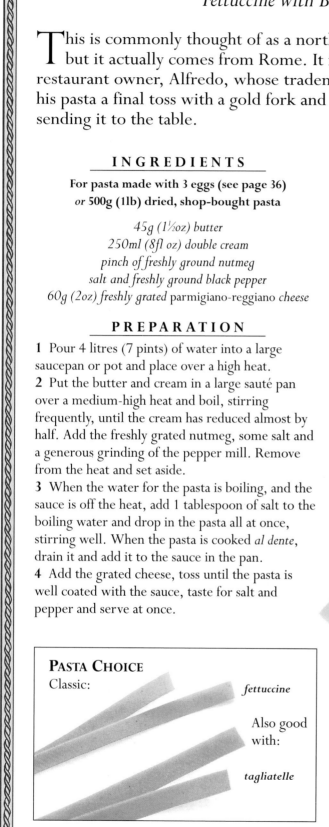

Butter

Double cream

PASTA CHOICE
Classic:

fettuccine

Also good with:

tagliatelle

Fettuccine all'Alfredo

Parmigiano-
reggiano

Black pepper

Nutmeg

Salt

SPAGHETTI ALLA
CARBONARA

Spaghetti with Pancetta and Raw Eggs

Many recipes I've seen for this dish call for cream. The way I learned to make it from my mother is without cream and this is still the way I prefer it – I find the creaminess from the eggs and cheese in contact with the hot pasta is enough. But I deviate from my mother's recipe in using just the yolk rather than the whole egg, which makes the dish a little richer. If *pancetta* is unavailable you can substitute good quality, lean bacon. It should be unsmoked.

INGREDIENTS

For 500g (1lb) dried, shop-bought pasta

30g (1oz) butter
30ml (2 tbsps) extra-virgin olive oil
125g (4oz) pancetta, cut from a 6mm (¼in) thick slice into thin strips
90ml (6 tbsps) dry white wine
4 egg yolks
3 tbsps freshly grated parmigiano-reggiano cheese
1 tbsp freshly grated pecorino romano cheese
1 tbsp finely chopped flat-leaf parsley
salt and freshly ground black pepper

PREPARATION

1 Pour 4 litres (7 pints) of water into a large saucepan or pot and place over a high heat.
2 Put the butter and olive oil in a small sauté pan over a medium-high heat. When the butter has melted, add the *pancetta* and cook until it is well browned but not crisp. Pour in the white wine and continue cooking until it has reduced by about half. Remove from the heat and set aside.
3 When the water for the pasta is boiling, and the sauce is off the heat, add 1 tablespoon of salt to the boiling water and drop in the pasta all at once, stirring until the strands are submerged.
4 In a mixing bowl (large enough to accommodate the pasta), lightly beat the egg yolks with the two grated cheeses, the parsley, a pinch of salt and several grindings of the pepper mill.
5 When the pasta is cooked *al dente*, return the pan with the *pancetta* to a high heat, then drain the pasta and add it to the mixing bowl containing the egg yolks and cheese. Toss until the pasta is well coated with the egg and cheese mixture and add the hot *pancetta*. Serve at once.

White wine

Pancetta

Extra-virgin olive oil

Butter

PASTA CHOICE
Classic:

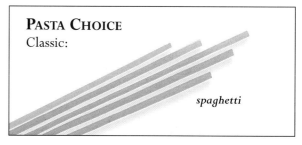

spaghetti

Egg yolks

Parmigiano-reggiano

Pecorino romano

Flat-leaf parsley

Salt

Black pepper

**Spaghetti
alla carbonara**

SPAGHETTI ALLE
VONGOLE

Spaghetti with Clams

The trick to getting the best flavour in this dish is to finish cooking the *spaghetti* in the pan along with the sauce so it absorbs the juices that the clams gave off as they steamed open. The clams that take the longest to steam open in the pan are the freshest – don't discard them. Do, however, discard clams that are open when you buy them and don't snap shut if you tap them; they are dead.

INGREDIENTS

For 500g (1lb) dried, shop-bought pasta

90ml (6 tbsps) extra-virgin olive oil
1 tsp finely chopped garlic
1 tbsp finely chopped flat-leaf parsley
small pinch of crushed chillies
48 live baby clams, soaked for 5 minutes
and rinsed, shells scoured
salt
90ml (6 tbsps) dry white wine
30g (1oz) butter

PREPARATION

1 Put the olive oil and garlic in a large sauté pan (large enough to accommodate the clams and the pasta later) over a medium-high heat and cook until the garlic begins to sizzle. Then stir in the crushed chillies and the parsley.
2 Add the clams in their shells, season with salt and stir well. Pour in the wine and cook, stirring occasionally, until the alcohol has bubbled away: about 1 minute. Then cover the pan to steam the clams open.
3 While the clams are steaming, pour 4 litres (7 pints) of water into a large saucepan or pot and place over a high heat.
4 Check the clams frequently, and when they have all opened, remove the pan from the heat.
5 When the water for the pasta is boiling, add 1 tablespoon of salt and drop in the pasta all at once, stirring until the strands are submerged. When the pasta is *molto al dente* (about 1 minute away from being *al dente)*, drain it.
6 Immediately, return the clams to a medium heat and add the drained pasta so that it finishes cooking in the pan. By the time it is *al dente* there should be very little liquid left (you can control this by covering or uncovering the pan as the pasta cooks). Swirl in the butter and serve at once.

Crushed chillies

Flat-leaf parsley

Garlic

Extra-virgin olive oil

PASTA CHOICE
Classic:

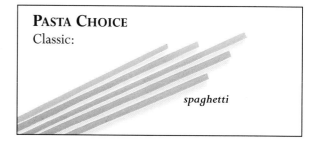

spaghetti

Clams

Salt

White wine

Butter

Spaghetti alle vongole

RECIPES

The recipes in this chapter, both classic and new, are grouped according to type and shape of pasta. All express the genuine and direct approach to flavour that is characteristic of Italian cooking. You will find hot and cold dishes, soups, and even a dessert. Each recipe is presented with its ideal choice of pasta shape, with suggestions for suitable alternatives.

Each recipe serves 6 people if followed by a second course, or 4 people if served on its own

For a step-by-step guide to preparing vegetables, see pages 150–1

PASTA LUNGA

Long Pasta

SPAGHETTINI ALLE ERBE

Spaghettini with Garlic and Fresh Herbs

This is a good example of how breadcrumbs are sometimes used with olive oil-based sauces to help the sauce cling to the pasta.

INGREDIENTS

For 500g (1lb) *spaghettini*

120ml (8 tbsps) extra-virgin olive oil
1 tsp finely chopped garlic
2 tbsps finely chopped flat-leaf parsley
½ tsp finely chopped fresh rosemary
½ tsp finely chopped fresh thyme
salt and freshly ground black pepper
1 tsp shredded fresh basil
2 tbsps plain dried breadcrumbs

PREPARATION

1 Bring 4 litres (7 pints) of water to the boil in a large saucepan or pot, add 1 tablespoon of salt and drop in the pasta all at once, stirring until the strands are submerged.
2 Put the olive oil and garlic in a large sauté pan over a medium-high heat and cook until the garlic begins to change colour.
3 Stir in the parsley, rosemary and thyme and season with salt and black pepper. After about 30 seconds, remove from the heat and set aside.
4 When the pasta is cooked *al dente*, drain it and add it to the sauce in the pan, and return the pan to a low heat.
5 Add the basil and toss until the pasta is well coated with the sauce. Sprinkle the breadcrumbs over, toss again, taste for salt and serve at once.

Also good with: *spaghetti*

SPAGHETTINI ALLA NURSINA

Spaghettini with Black Truffles

This dish is named after Norcia, a town in the heart of black-truffle country in central Italy. Although the white truffle from Alba is the aristocrat of truffles, the black truffle is certainly not to be scoffed at. I cannot think of a better way to eat spaghettini *than enveloped in the rich woodsy aroma and flavour of black truffles.*

INGREDIENTS

For 500g (1lb) *spaghettini*

120ml (8 tbsps) extra-virgin olive oil
2–3 cloves garlic, lightly crushed and peeled but kept whole
2 anchovy fillets, finely chopped
125–150g (4–5oz) fresh **or**, *if very good quality, preserved black truffles, finely grated*
salt

PREPARATION

1 Bring 4 litres (7 pints) of water to the boil in a large saucepan or pot, add 1 tablespoon of salt and drop in the pasta all at once, stirring until the strands are submerged.
2 Put the olive oil and garlic in a large sauté pan over a medium-high heat and cook until the garlic has browned on all sides.
3 Remove and discard the garlic and turn the heat down to low. Allow the oil to cool slightly, then add the anchovies. Cook, stirring with a wooden spoon, until the anchovies have dissolved completely. Remove the pan from the heat, stir in the truffles and season very lightly with salt.
4 When the pasta is cooked *al dente*, drain and toss thoroughly with the sauce. Taste for salt and serve at once.

Spaghettini ai Gamberi, Pomodoro e Capperi

Spaghettini with Prawns, Tomatoes and Capers

INGREDIENTS

For 500g (1lb) *spaghettini*

90ml (6 tbsps) extra-virgin olive oil
125g (4oz) onion, thinly sliced lengthways
500g (1lb) fresh ripe plum tomatoes, peeled, seeded
and cut into 1cm (½in) dice
½ tsp chopped fresh oregano or ¼ tsp dried
1½ tbsps capers
350g (12oz) medium-sized raw prawns, peeled, deveined
if necessary, and cut into 1cm (½in) pieces
salt and freshly ground black pepper

PREPARATION

1 Put the olive oil and onion in a large sauté pan over a medium heat and cook until the onion has turned golden brown at the edges.

2 Raise the heat to medium-high and add the tomatoes. Cook rapidly until most of the liquid has evaporated but the tomatoes have not broken down completely. You may need to raise the heat even more for this but take care not to burn them.

3 Meanwhile, bring 4 litres (7 pints) of water to the boil in a large saucepan or pot, add 1 tablespoon of salt and drop in the pasta all at once, stirring until the strands are submerged.

4 Add the oregano, capers and prawns to the sauce in the pan and season with salt and black pepper. Cook until the prawns turn pink, about 2 minutes, then remove the pan from the heat.

5 When the pasta is cooked *al dente*, drain and toss with the sauce. Serve at once.

Also good with: *spaghetti*

SPAGHETTINI ALLE OLIVE NERE

Spaghettini with Tomatoes and Black Olives

INGREDIENTS

For 500g (1lb) *spaghettini*

90ml (6 tbsps) extra-virgin olive oil
2 tsps finely chopped garlic
2 tbsps finely chopped flat-leaf parsley
500g (1lb) tinned whole peeled tomatoes, with their juice, coarsely chopped
salt and freshly ground black pepper
8 – 10 black olives, flesh sliced from around stone

PREPARATION

1 Put the olive oil and garlic in a saucepan over a medium-high heat and cook until the garlic begins to change colour.

2 Stir in the parsley then add the tomatoes. Season with salt and black pepper and cook until the tomatoes have reduced and separated from the oil. Remove from the heat and set aside.

You can prepare the sauce ahead of time up to this point and refrigerate or even freeze it.

3 Bring 4 litres (7 pints) of water to the boil in a large saucepan or pot, add 1 tablespoon of salt and drop in the pasta all at once, stirring until the strands are submerged.

4 Return the pan with the sauce to a low heat and mix in the olives.

5 When the pasta is cooked *al dente*, drain and toss with the sauce. Taste for salt and pepper and serve at once.

Also good with: *spaghetti*

SPAGHETTI AI GAMBERI E PEPERONI ARROSTO

Spaghetti with Prawns and Roasted Red Peppers

INGREDIENTS

For 500g (1lb) *spaghetti*

2 red peppers
45ml (3 tbsps) extra-virgin olive oil
½ tsp finely chopped garlic
250g (8oz) medium-sized raw prawns, peeled, deveined if necessary, and cut into 1cm (½in) pieces
salt and freshly ground black pepper
180ml (6fl oz) double cream
1 tbsp finely chopped flat-leaf parsley

PREPARATION

1 Roast the red peppers under the grill or over an open flame until the skin is charred on all sides. Place them in a bowl and cover the bowl tightly with cling film. After about 20 minutes take the peppers out, cut them in half, remove the core and scrape away the blistered skin and the seeds. Cut the flesh into 2cm (¾in) squares.

2 Bring 4 litres (7 pints) of water to the boil in a large saucepan or pot, add 1 tablespoon of salt and drop in the pasta all at once, stirring until the strands are submerged.

3 Put the olive oil and garlic in a large sauté pan over a medium-high heat and cook until the garlic begins to change colour. Add the prawns, season with salt and black pepper and sauté, stirring frequently, until the prawns have turned pink: 1 – 2 minutes.

4 Stir in the roasted peppers and add the cream and the parsley. Cook until the cream has reduced by at least half, then remove the pan from the heat and set aside.

5 When the pasta is cooked *al dente*, return the pan with the sauce to a low heat, drain the pasta and add it to the pan. Toss over the heat until the pasta is well coated. Serve at once.

Also good with: *fusilli lunghi, fettuccine*

SPAGHETTINI AI GAMBERI E FINOCCHIO

Spaghettini with Prawns and Fresh Fennel

INGREDIENTS

For 500g (1lb) *spaghettini*

90ml (6 tbsps) extra-virgin olive oil
2 tsps finely chopped garlic
*350g (12oz) fresh fennel, tops removed, bulbs sliced
very thinly lengthways*
*500g (1lb) fresh ripe plum tomatoes, peeled, seeded
and cut into 1cm (½in) dice*
1 tsp chopped fresh marjoram or ½ tsp dried
*350g (12oz) medium-sized raw prawns, peeled, deveined
if necessary, and cut into 1cm (½in) pieces*
salt and freshly ground black pepper

PREPARATION

1 Put the olive oil and garlic in a large sauté pan over a medium-high heat and cook until the garlic begins to change colour. Stir in the fennel, coating it well with the oil, and add about 50ml (3 tbsps) of water. Turn the heat down to medium-low, cover the pan and cook until the fennel is very tender: about 15–25 minutes.
2 Pour 4 litres (7 pints) of water into a large saucepan or pot and place over a high heat.
3 Uncover the pan with the fennel, raise the heat to medium-high, and cook until any water in the pan has evaporated. Stir in the tomatoes and cook briefly until the water they release has evaporated.
4 When the water for the pasta is boiling, add 1 tablespoon of salt and drop in the pasta all at once, stirring until the strands are submerged.
5 Add the marjoram and the prawns to the sauce, season with salt and black pepper, and cook until the prawns have turned pink: about 2 minutes. Remove the pan from the heat and set aside.
6 When the pasta is cooked *al dente*, drain and toss with the sauce. Taste for salt and pepper and serve at once.

Also good with: *spaghetti, fusilli lunghi*

SPAGHETTI AL SUGO DI CIPOLLE VARIE

Spaghetti with Leeks, Shallots and Red Onions

INGREDIENTS

For 500g (1lb) *spaghetti*

120ml (8 tbsps) extra-virgin olive oil
4 tbsps thinly sliced shallots
250g (8oz) red onions, thinly sliced
*350g (12oz) leeks, green tops removed, cut into thin
strips 5cm (2in) long*
salt and freshly ground black pepper
60ml (4 tbsps) dry white wine
2 tbsps finely chopped flat-leaf parsley
6 tbsps freshly grated parmigiano-reggiano *cheese*

PREPARATION

1 Put the olive oil and shallots in a large sauté pan over a medium heat and cook until the shallots are lightly coloured.
2 Stir in the onions and leeks, season generously with salt and black pepper, add 60ml (4 tbsps) water, turn the heat down to medium-low and cover the pan. Cook until the onions and leeks have softened and become very tender: about 20–30 minutes.
3 Pour 4 litres (7 pints) of water into a large saucepan or pot and place over a high heat.
4 Uncover the pan with the sauce and raise the heat to medium-high. Cook, stirring occasionally, until any liquid in the pan has evaporated and the onions and leeks start to turn a rich golden colour.
5 When the water for the pasta is boiling, add 1 tablespoon of salt and drop in the pasta all at once, stirring until the strands are submerged.
6 Add the wine and parsley to the sauce and cook until the wine has evaporated almost completely. Remove the pan from the heat and set aside.
7 When the pasta is cooked *al dente*, drain and toss with the sauce, adding the grated cheese. Taste for salt and pepper and serve at once.

Also good with: *spaghettini, tonnarelli, fusilli lunghi*

FUSILLI LUNGHI ALLA RUSTICA

Long Fusilli with Peppers, Olives and Vegetables

This zesty, flavourful sauce is a recipe of my mother's that I am very fond of and have made minor changes to.

INGREDIENTS

For 500g (1lb) *fusilli lunghi*

120ml (8 tbsps) extra-virgin olive oil
350g (12oz) onion, thinly sliced
1 tsp finely chopped garlic
½ tsp crushed chillies
2 tbsps finely chopped flat-leaf parsley
90g (3oz) pancetta, cut from a 6mm (¼in) thick slice into thin strips
1 large yellow or red pepper or ½ of each, cored and seeded, peeled and cut into strips 1cm (½in) wide
500g (1lb) fresh ripe plum tomatoes, peeled, seeded and cut into 1cm (½in) dice
salt
90g (3oz) green olives, flesh sliced from around stone
2 tbsps capers
1 tsp coarsely chopped fresh oregano or ½ tsp dried
2 tbsps fresh basil leaves, torn by hand into small pieces
4 tbsps freshly grated parmigiano-reggiano cheese
2 tbsps freshly grated pecorino romano cheese

PREPARATION

1 Put the olive oil and onion in a large sauté pan over a medium-low heat and cook until the onion has softened and turned a rich golden colour.
2 Raise the heat to medium-high and stir in the garlic, crushed chillies and parsley. Sauté for about 30 seconds. Add the *pancetta* and cook until it is lightly browned but not crisp.
3 Pour 4 litres (7 pints) of water into a large saucepan or pot and place over a high heat.
4 Add the strips of pepper to the sauté pan with the sauce and cook, stirring occasionally, until they are tender: about 5–6 minutes. Put in the tomatoes and cook until they are no longer watery: about another 5–6 minutes.
5 Season with salt, stir in the olives, capers, oregano and basil, and after about 30 seconds remove from the heat and set aside.
6 When the water for the pasta is boiling, add 1 tablespoon of salt and drop in the pasta all at once, stirring until the strands are submerged.
7 When the pasta is cooked *al dente*, drain and toss with the sauce, adding the grated cheeses. Taste for salt and serve at once.

Also good with: *fusilli corti, penne, elicoidali*

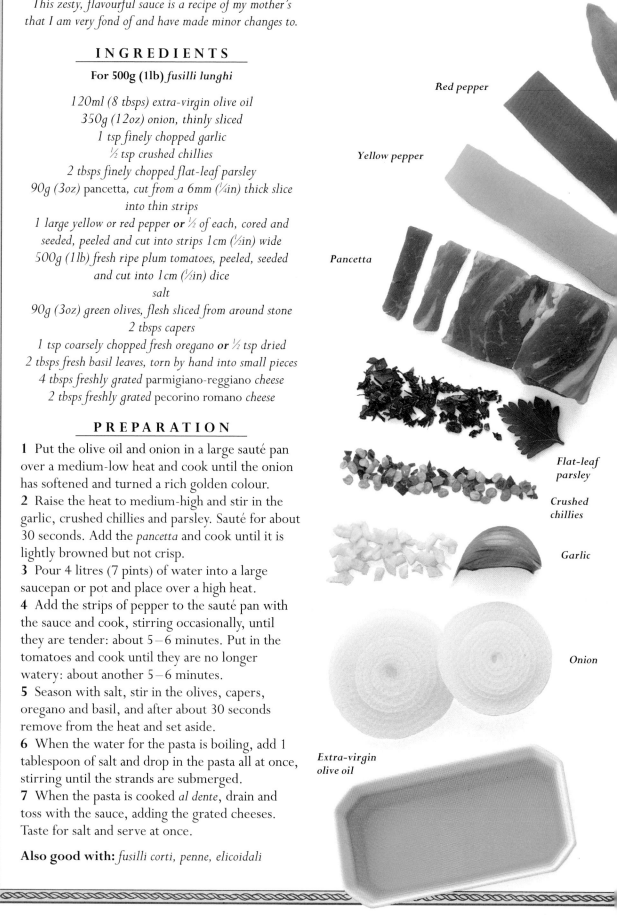

Red pepper

Yellow pepper

Pancetta

Flat-leaf parsley

Crushed chillies

Garlic

Onion

Extra-virgin olive oil

Fresh plum
tomatoes

Salt

Green
olives

Capers

Oregano

Basil

Parmigiano-
reggiano

Pecorino
romano

Fusilli
lunghi

**Fusilli lunghi
alla rustica**

SPAGHETTI AI FRUTTI DI MARE

Spaghetti with Seafood Sauce

With two long coastlines, Italy has a wealth of seafood pasta dishes. This is one of the more common ones, a shellfish lover's delight that is found along both coasts, the Adriatic and the Mediterranean.

INGREDIENTS

For 500g (1lb) *spaghetti*

350g (12oz) squid
12 live baby clams in their shells
12 live mussels in their shells
125g (4oz) loose scallops, without coral
125g (4oz) medium-sized raw prawns
90ml (6 tbsps) extra-virgin olive oil, plus a little extra to add to the sauce
1 tsp finely chopped garlic
1 tbsp finely chopped flat-leaf parsley
75ml (5 tbsps) white wine
500g (1lb) tinned whole peeled tomatoes, with their juice, coarsely chopped
salt
⅛ tsp crushed chillies

PREPARATION

1 Prepare the squid as shown, then cut the tentacles in half and the bodies into rings.
2 Clean the baby clams and mussels: soak them in water for 5 minutes, rinse them, and scour the shells. Discard any that are open. Remove the beards from the mussels, and remove the coral from the scallops if it is there. Peel and devein the prawns and cut in half.
3 Put the olive oil and garlic in a large sauté pan over a medium-high heat and cook until the garlic begins to sizzle. Then stir in the parsley and the squid, and continue stirring for 1–2 minutes.
4 Pour in the white wine and continue cooking until it has reduced by half.
5 Add the tomatoes and bring to the boil, then reduce the heat to low, cover the pan with the lid on loosely and simmer until the squid is very tender: about 45 minutes. If the liquid evaporates before the squid is done, pour in a little water.
6 When the squid is tender, add some salt (do not add salt before this point or the squid will become tough) and set the pan aside.
7 Bring 4 litres (7 pints) of water to the boil in a large saucepan or pot, add 1 tablespoon of salt and drop in the pasta all at once, stirring until the strands are submerged.

PREPARING SQUID

1 *Rinse the squid first. Then remove the inner sac by pulling the head and body apart. The inner sac comes away with the head.*

8 Return the sauce to the heat and put in the crushed chillies. Add the clams and mussels, and when they begin to open (after about 2 minutes), add the scallops and the prawns. Season with salt, pour in a little extra olive oil, and cook for 2–3 minutes more. Set aside.
9 When the pasta is cooked *al dente*, drain and toss thoroughly with the sauce in a serving bowl, leaving the clams and mussels in their shells. Taste for salt and serve at once.

Clams

Prawn

Mussel

Scallop

2 Detach the tentacles from the head and inner sac by cutting above the eyes. Keep the tentacles, which are edible, but discard the rest.

3 You need to remove the beak from the tentacles. Feel for the hard lump then gently work it out of the flesh by squeezing it.

4 Discard the transparent backbone then peel off the skin (this is easiest done under running water). Rinse again.

Spaghetti ai frutti di mare

LINGUINE AL SUGO DI VONGOLE E ZUCCHINE

Linguine with Clams and Courgettes

Courgettes and seafood are an inspired combination, and one that is often found along the coast near Naples. Despite their popularity outside the country, linguine are not widely used in Italian cooking, but their shape and sturdiness make them an ideal choice for this sauce.

INGREDIENTS

For 500g (1lb) *linguine*

120ml (8 tbsps) extra-virgin olive oil
100g (3½oz) finely chopped onion
2 tsps finely chopped garlic
500g (1lb) small courgettes, trimmed and cut into 1cm (½in) dice
salt and freshly ground black pepper
90ml (6 tbsps) dry white wine
36–48 (depending on size) live baby clams, soaked for 5 minutes and rinsed, shells scoured
2 tbsps fresh basil leaves, torn by hand into small pieces

PREPARATION

1 Put the olive oil and onion in a large sauté pan (large enough to accommodate the clams and the pasta later) over a medium-high heat and sauté until the onion softens and turns golden in colour.
2 Add the garlic and sauté until it begins to colour, then stir in the courgettes, season with salt and black pepper and reduce the heat to medium. Cook, stirring occasionally, until the courgettes are tender and lightly coloured.
3 Pour 4 litres (7 pints) of water into a large saucepan or pot and place over a high heat.
4 Turn the heat up to medium-high under the sauté pan and pour in the white wine. Let the wine cook until the alcohol has bubbled away: about 1 minute. Meanwhile, go through the cleaned clams, discarding any that are open.
5 Put the closed clams in the sauté pan. Stir well and cover the pan to steam them open (those that take longest to open are the freshest). Check them frequently and, when all the clams have opened, remove the pan from the heat.
6 When the water for the pasta is boiling, add 1 tablespoon of salt and drop in the pasta all at once, stirring until the strands are submerged.
7 When the pasta is *molto al dente* (about 1 minute away from being *al dente*), return the pan with the clams to a medium heat, drain the pasta and add it to the clams. (It will finish cooking in the pan.)

8 Sprinkle the basil over the pasta, add up to 60ml (4 tbsps) of water if there is only a little clam juice left, cover and cook until the pasta is *al dente*. The finished dish should be moist, but if it is too runny, uncover the pan and raise the heat until the excess liquid has evaporated. Serve at once.

Also good with: *spaghetti (but not quite so successful)*

SPAGHETTI ALLA FIORETTO

Spaghetti with Marinated Halibut

My wife and I discovered this surprising recipe in a restaurant called Fioretto in Latina, a town south of Rome. The sauce never sees the inside of a pan, nor gets exposed to heat, but the fish is "cooked" by being marinated in lemon juice. A boiled potato is mixed in at the end to thicken the sauce and help it bind to the pasta. The result is a delightful and refreshing dish, perfect for summer.

INGREDIENTS

For 500g (1lb) *spaghetti*

350g (12oz) halibut fillet, boned and cut into 1cm (½in) dice
90ml (6 tbsps) lemon juice
4 tbsps finely chopped red onion
¼ tsp crushed chillies
2 tbsps finely chopped flat-leaf parsley
120ml (8 tbsps) extra-virgin olive oil
salt
½ large boiling potato, peeled

PREPARATION

1 Put all the ingredients in a mixing bowl except for the potato. Season generously with salt and mix well. Leave at room temperature, stirring occasionally, for a minimum of 2 hours, or until the fish has "cooked" and lost its raw look.
2 When the fish is ready, prepare the potato by boiling it until it is very soft.
3 Bring 4 litres (7 pints) of water to the boil in a large saucepan or pot, add 1 tablespoon of salt and drop in the pasta all at once, stirring until the strands are submerged.
4 Mash the boiled potato and add it to the bowl with the sauce, mixing it in thoroughly.
5 When the pasta is cooked *al dente*, drain it and add it to the bowl, tossing vigorously until the pasta is well coated. Taste for salt and add a little extra olive oil if the sauce is dry. Serve at once.

SPAGHETTI AL TONNO FRESCO

Spaghetti with Fresh Tuna and Roasted Peppers

INGREDIENTS

For 500g (1lb) *spaghetti*

2 red peppers
90ml (6 tbsps) extra-virgin olive oil
60g (2oz) thinly sliced onion
1 tsp finely chopped garlic
250g (8oz) fresh tuna, cut into 1cm (½in) chunks
salt and freshly ground black pepper
60ml (4 tbsps) dry white wine
1 tbsp finely chopped flat-leaf parsley
2 tbsps capers

PREPARATION

1 Roast the red peppers under the grill or over an open flame until the skin is charred on all sides. Place them in a bowl and cover the bowl tightly with cling film. After about 20 minutes take the peppers out, cut them in half, remove the core and scrape away the blistered skin and the seeds. Cut them into strips 4cm (about 1½in) long and 6mm (¼in) wide.
2 Pour 4 litres (7 pints) of water into a large saucepan or pot and place over a high heat.
3 Put the olive oil and onion in a large sauté pan over a medium-low heat and cook until the onion has softened and turned a rich golden colour at the edges.
4 Turn the heat up to medium-high and add the garlic. Cook for about 1 minute, then add the tuna. Cook, stirring often, for another minute or until the tuna has lost its raw colour. Take care not to overcook the tuna or it will be too dry. Season with salt and black pepper.
5 When the water for the pasta is boiling, add 1 tablespoon of salt and drop in the pasta all at once, stirring until the strands are submerged.
6 Add the roasted peppers to the tuna, stir for about 30 seconds, then pour in the wine. Once the wine has reduced, stir in the parsley and capers. Remove from the heat.
7 When the pasta is cooked *al dente*, drain and toss with the sauce. Taste for salt and pepper and serve at once.

Also good with: *fusilli lunghi, spaghettini*

SPAGHETTI ALLE COZZE

Spaghetti with Mussels

INGREDIENTS

For 500g (1lb) *spaghetti*

90ml (6 tbsps) extra-virgin olive oil
1 tsp finely chopped garlic
⅛ tsp crushed chillies
1 tbsp finely chopped flat-leaf parsley
60ml (4 tbsps) dry white wine
500g (1lb) fresh ripe plum tomatoes, peeled, seeded and cut into 1cm (½in) dice
salt
40 live mussels in their shells, soaked for 5 minutes and rinsed, shells scoured, beards removed
2 tbsps freshly shredded basil

PREPARATION

1 Pour 4 litres (7 pints) of water into a large saucepan or pot and place over a high heat.
2 Put 60ml (4 tbsps) of the olive oil and all the garlic in a large sauté pan (large enough to accommodate the mussels and the pasta later) over a medium-high heat and cook until the garlic begins to sizzle. Then stir in the crushed chillies and the parsley and pour in the wine.
3 Once the alcohol from the wine has bubbled away, about 1 minute, add the tomatoes and season with salt. Go through the cleaned mussels, discarding any that are open, and put the closed ones in with the tomatoes. Stir well and cover the pan to steam them open (those that take the longest to open are the freshest).
4 When the water for the pasta is boiling, add 1 tablespoon of salt and drop in the pasta all at once, stirring until the strands are submerged.
5 Check the mussels frequently, and when they have all opened, stir in the basil and remove the pan from the heat.
6 When the pasta is *molto al dente* (about 1 minute away from being *al dente*), return the pan with the mussels to a medium heat, drain the pasta and add it to the mussels so that it finishes cooking in the pan. When it is *al dente* there should be very little liquid left (you can control this by covering or uncovering the pan as the pasta cooks).
7 Stir in the remaining olive oil and serve at once with the mussels in their shells.

Spaghetti alle cozze
(page 81)

Bucatini alla sorrentina
(page 84)

Spaghetti al tonno fresco
(page 81)

BUCATINI ALLA SORRENTINA

Bucatini with Tomatoes, Basil and Mozzarella

From the region of Campania, known for its sweet and flavourful tomatoes and its rich fresh buffalo-milk mozzarella, comes this delightful recipe. Unless you can find fresh tomatoes as good as those of Campania it is best to use good quality tinned ones. Buffalo-milk mozzarella can also be difficult to find, and is very expensive, so I recommend using a good cow's milk mozzarella instead, made with full-cream milk.

INGREDIENTS

For 500g (1lb) *bucatini*

60g (2oz) butter
125g (4oz) thinly sliced onion
500g (1lb) tinned whole peeled tomatoes, with their juice, coarsely chopped
salt and freshly ground black pepper
2 tbsps fresh basil leaves, torn by hand into small pieces
250g (8oz) full-cream Italian mozzarella, cut into 6mm (¼in) dice

PREPARATION

1 Melt the butter in a saucepan over a medium heat. Add the onion and cook until it has softened and turned a rich golden colour.
2 Add the tomatoes, season with salt and black pepper and cook until the tomatoes have reduced and separated from the butter: 15–25 minutes.

You can prepare the sauce ahead of time up to this point and refrigerate or even freeze it.

3 Stir in the basil and cook for about 2 minutes. Remove from the heat and set aside.
4 Bring 4 litres (7 pints) of water to the boil in a large saucepan or pot, add 1 tablespoon of salt and drop in the pasta all at once, stirring until the strands are submerged.
5 After the pasta has cooked for 5 minutes, return the pan with the sauce to a low heat. When the pasta is *molto al dente* (about 30 seconds away from being *al dente*), drain and transfer to a serving bowl. Add the sauce and the *mozzarella*. Cover the bowl with a plate and allow to stand for 2–3 minutes so the cheese melts before you serve it.

Also good with: *fusilli lunghi, spaghetti*

BUCATINI ALL'AMATRICIANA

Bucatini with Spicy Tomato Sauce

This is a classic Roman dish. If you order it in a restaurant in Rome you may find that when the waiter brings the dish to your table he covers it with a plate and goes away. You will wonder why, because covering a dish of pasta is usually the worst thing you can do to it. But he knows exactly what he's doing — with the steam trapped in, the hot pasta becomes infused with the spiciness of the chillies.

INGREDIENTS

For 500g (1lb) *bucatini*

60g (2oz) butter
100g (3½oz) finely chopped onion
60g (2oz) pancetta, cut from a 1cm (½in) thick slice into thin strips
500g (1lb) tinned whole peeled tomatoes, with their juice, coarsely chopped
¼ tsp or more crushed chillies
salt
6 tbsps freshly grated parmigiano-reggiano cheese
2 tbsps freshly grated pecorino romano cheese

PREPARATION

1 Melt half the butter in a saucepan over a medium-low heat. Add the onion and cook until it turns a rich golden colour. Add the *pancetta* and sauté until it is lightly browned but not crisp.
2 Stir in the tomatoes and crushed chillies and season with salt. Cook until the tomatoes have reduced and separated from the butter: 20–30 minutes. Remove from the heat and set aside.

You may prepare the sauce ahead of time up to this point and refrigerate it.

3 Bring 4 litres (7 pints) of water to the boil in a large saucepan or pot, add 1 tablespoon of salt and drop in the pasta all at once, stirring until the strands are submerged.
4 After the pasta has cooked for 5 minutes, return the pan with the sauce to a low heat. When the pasta is *molto al dente* (about 30 seconds away from being *al dente*), drain and transfer to a serving bowl. Add the sauce, the remaining butter and the grated cheeses and toss vigorously. Cover the bowl and wait 2 minutes before serving.

Also good with: *fusilli lunghi, penne lisce*

BUCATINI COI POMODORI AL FORNO

Bucatini with Oven-Baked Tomatoes

Oven-baked tomatoes have been a family favourite for as long as I can remember, and appeared in my mother's first book. My mother often included them in a sandwich as part of my school lunch when I was a child in New York — to the surprise of my classmates, who unwrapped sandwiches filled with ham and cheese as I unwrapped ones of veal cutlet, fried aubergine and oven-baked tomatoes. A delicious way to have these tomatoes is as a sauce for pasta.

INGREDIENTS

For 500g (1lb) *bucatini*

*350g (12oz) fresh ripe plum tomatoes
1 tbsp finely chopped garlic
2 tbsps finely chopped flat-leaf parsley
salt and freshly ground black pepper
90ml (6 tbsps) extra-virgin olive oil
2 tbsps freshly grated* pecorino romano *cheese
4 tbsps freshly grated* parmigiano-reggiano *cheese*

PREPARATION

1 Preheat the oven to 180°C/350°F/gas 4.
2 Cut the tomatoes in half lengthways, remove the seeds and place the halves in a baking tin with the cut side up. Sprinkle the garlic and parsley into the cavities and season with salt and black pepper. Drizzle the olive oil over the tomatoes and put the tin in the oven. Bake until the tomatoes have shrivelled slightly and begun to brown at the edges: about 1 hour. Save the oil from the pan.

You can prepare the tomatoes ahead of time and refrigerate them.

3 Bring 4 litres (7 pints) of water to the boil in a large saucepan or pot, add 1 tablespoon of salt and drop in the pasta all at once, stirring until the strands are submerged.
4 Meanwhile, when the tomatoes are cool enough to handle, scrape the flesh away from the skin with a knife. Discard the skins and coarsely chop the flesh. Put the chopped tomatoes and the reserved olive oil into a saucepan over a medium-low heat. Stir from time to time while the pasta cooks.
5 When the pasta is cooked *al dente*, drain and toss with the sauce and the two grated cheeses. Serve at once.

Also good with: *spaghetti, penne, fusilli lunghi, fusilli corti, penne, cavatappi*

SPAGHETTI FREDDI COI FRUTTI DI MARE

Spaghetti Salad with Prawns and Scallops

To an Italian, eating cold pasta is usually considered an unnatural act, but, although exceedingly rare, cold pasta dishes do exist in Italy. They bear no resemblance, however, to the distorted interpretations outside Italy. You would never find, for example, sweet mayonnaise-type dressings. Italian pasta salads are meant to provide a refreshing, palate-stimulating defence against the appetite-deadening heat of a midsummer day.

INGREDIENTS

For 500g (1lb) *spaghetti*

*2 red peppers
salt
30ml (2 tbsps) red wine vinegar
125g (4oz) medium-sized raw prawns
125g (4oz) loose scallops, without coral
75ml (5 tbsps) extra-virgin olive oil
12 green olives, flesh sliced from around stone
12 black olives, flesh sliced from around stone
2 tsps finely chopped fresh marjoram or ⅓ tsp dried
2 tbsps finely chopped flat-leaf parsley
¼ tsp crushed chillies
30ml (2 tbsps) freshly squeezed lemon juice*

PREPARATION

1 Roast the red peppers under the grill or over an open flame until the skin is charred on all sides. Place them in a bowl and cover the bowl tightly with cling film. After about 20 minutes take the peppers out, cut them in half, remove the core and scrape away the blistered skin and the seeds. Cut the flesh into 1cm (½in) squares.
2 Bring 2 litres (3½ pints) of water to the boil, add 2 teaspoons of salt and the vinegar and drop in the prawns. When they have turned pink and the water has returned to the boil (1–2 minutes), remove them with a slotted spoon and set aside. Drop in the scallops. When the scallops are cooked (2–3 minutes), drain them.
3 When cool enough to handle, peel the prawns. Cut the prawns and scallops into 1cm (½in) pieces.
4 Bring 4 litres (7 pints) of water to the boil, add 1 tablespoon of salt and drop in the pasta all at once, stirring until the strands are submerged.
5 When the pasta is *molto al dente* (about 30 seconds away from being *al dente*), drain and toss in a bowl with 30ml (2 tbsps) of the olive oil until it is well coated. Add all the rest of the ingredients and toss well. Allow to cool completely before serving but do not refrigerate.

SPAGHETTI ALLA CHECCA

Spaghetti with Fresh Tomatoes, Herbs and Mozzarella

I discovered this refreshing summer dish at a restaurant called Cambusa in Positano, near Naples. It is another of those "uncooked" sauces where the ingredients are simply scalded with hot oil before being tossed with the pasta.

INGREDIENTS

For 500g (1lb) *spaghetti*

1kg (2lb) fresh ripe plum tomatoes, peeled, seeded and cut into 6mm (¼in) dice
250g (8oz) full-cream Italian mozzarella, cut into 6mm (¼in) dice
2 tsps chopped fresh basil
2 tsps chopped fresh oregano
2 tsps chopped fresh marjoram
1 tsp chopped fresh thyme
salt and freshly ground black pepper
120ml (8 tbsps) extra-virgin olive oil

PREPARATION

1 Bring 4 litres (7 pints) of water to the boil in a large saucepan or pot, add 1 tablespoon of salt and drop in the pasta all at once, stirring until the strands are submerged.
2 Meanwhile, put the tomatoes, *mozzarella* and all the herbs in a serving bowl large enough to accommodate the pasta later. Season with salt and black pepper and mix well.
3 Heat the olive oil until it is smoking hot and pour it over the mixture in the bowl.
4 When the pasta is cooked *molto al dente* (about 30 seconds away from being *al dente*), drain and add to the sauce in the bowl. Toss vigorously until the pasta is well coated. Cover the bowl with a plate and allow to stand for 2 minutes so the cheese melts before you serve it.

Also good with: *spaghettini*

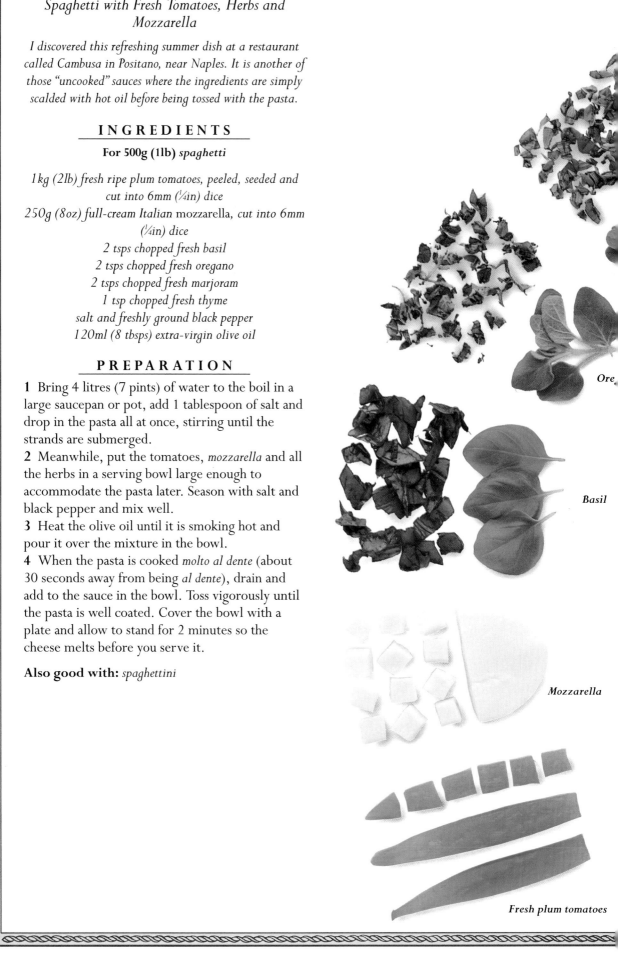

Ore

Basil

Mozzarella

Fresh plum tomatoes

Thyme

Salt

Black pepper

Extra-virgin olive oil

Spaghetti

Marjoram

Spaghetti alla checca

FUSILLI LUNGHI CON LA BELGA E PORRI

Long Fusilli with Chicory, Leeks and Roasted Red Pepper

INGREDIENTS

For 500g (1lb) *fusilli lunghi*

1 red pepper
90ml (6 tbsps) extra-virgin olive oil
1 tsp finely chopped garlic
3 medium-sized leeks, cut in half lengthways then across
into pieces 6mm (¼in) wide
60g (2oz) chicory, finely shredded lengthways
salt and freshly ground black pepper

PREPARATION

1 Roast the red pepper under the grill or over an open flame until the skin is charred on all sides. Place it in a bowl and cover the bowl tightly with cling film. After about 20 minutes take the pepper out, cut it in half, remove the core and scrape away the blistered skin and the seeds. Cut into strips 2.5cm (1in) long and 3mm (⅛in) wide.
2 Put the olive oil and garlic in a large sauté pan over a medium-high heat. When the garlic begins to change colour, add the leeks and chicory. Season with salt and black pepper, and stir well to coat with the oil and garlic. Turn the heat down to medium-low, cover the pan and cook, stirring occasionally, until the vegetables are very tender and almost creamy in texture: at least 20 minutes.
3 Meanwhile, bring 4 litres (7 pints) of water to the boil in a large saucepan or pot, add 1 tablespoon of salt and drop in the pasta all at once, stirring until the strands are submerged.
4 Uncover the pan of vegetables, raise the heat to medium-high and add the strips of roasted pepper. Cook, stirring frequently, for 2–3 minutes then remove from the heat and set aside.
5 When the pasta is cooked *al dente*, drain and toss with the sauce. Taste for salt and pepper and serve at once.

Also good with: *spaghetti, gnocchi, conchiglie*

SPAGHETTI AL POMODORO

Spaghetti with Tomatoes, Carrots and Celery

INGREDIENTS

For 500g (1lb) *spaghetti*

60g (2oz) butter
4 tbsps finely chopped onion
4 tbsps finely diced carrots
4 tbsps finely diced celery
500g (1lb) tinned whole peeled tomatoes, with
their juice, coarsely chopped
salt
6 tbsps freshly grated parmigiano-reggiano *cheese*

PREPARATION

1 Melt the butter in a saucepan over a medium-low heat. Add the onion and cook until it has softened and turned a rich golden colour. Add the carrots and celery and continue cooking until they are lightly coloured.
2 Pour in the tomatoes, season with salt and cook until they have reduced and separated from the butter: about 20–30 minutes. Remove from the heat and set aside.

You can prepare the sauce ahead of time up to this point and refrigerate or even freeze it.

3 Bring 4 litres (7 pints) of water to the boil, add 1 tablespoon of salt and drop in the pasta all at once, stirring until the strands are submerged.
4 When the pasta is almost done, return the sauce to a medium heat. Once the pasta is cooked *al dente*, drain and toss with the sauce, adding the grated cheese. Taste for salt and serve at once.

Also good with: *penne, fusilli lunghi, fusilli corti, spaghettini*

SPAGHETTI ALLA PUTTANESCA BIANCA

Spaghetti with Capers, Olives and Anchovies

This is known as a "white" puttanesca sauce because it is without tomatoes.

INGREDIENTS

For 500g (1lb) *spaghetti*

120ml (8 tbsps) extra-virgin olive oil
6 anchovy fillets, chopped
1 tsp finely chopped garlic
1 tbsp finely chopped flat-leaf parsley
2 tbsps capers
8 – 10 black olives, flesh sliced from around stone
salt
2 tbsps plain dried breadcrumbs

PREPARATION

1 Bring 4 litres (7 pints) of water to the boil in a large saucepan or pot, add 1 tablespoon of salt and drop in the pasta all at once, stirring until the strands are submerged.
2 Put the olive oil and anchovies in a large sauté pan over a medium heat and cook, stirring with a wooden spoon, until the anchovies have dissolved.
3 Add the garlic and sauté until it just begins to change colour.
4 Stir in the parsley, capers and olives, season with a little salt and cook for 1 – 2 minutes. Remove from the heat and set aside.
5 When the pasta is cooked *al dente*, drain and toss with the sauce, adding the breadcrumbs. Taste for salt and serve at once.

Also good with: *spaghettini*

SPAGHETTI AL COGNAC

Spaghetti with Fresh Tomatoes and Cognac

This dish was invented by Alfredo, the famous Roman chef who created Fettuccine all'Alfredo. *It is traditionally eaten in Rome at 4 a.m.*

INGREDIENTS

For 500g (1lb) *spaghetti*

90ml (6 tbsps) extra-virgin olive oil
175g (6oz) finely chopped onion
30ml (2 tbsps) cognac
500g (1lb) fresh ripe plum tomatoes, peeled, seeded and cut into 6mm (¼in) dice
salt and freshly ground black pepper

PREPARATION

1 Put the olive oil and onion in a large sauté pan over a medium heat and cook until the onion has softened and turned a rich golden colour.
2 Turn the heat up to medium-high and pour in the cognac. Cook for about 30 seconds to allow the alcohol to evaporate, then add the tomatoes. Season with salt and black pepper and cook, stirring occasionally, until the tomatoes have reduced and separated from the oil: about 10 – 20 minutes. Remove from the heat and set aside.
3 Bring 4 litres (7 pints) of water to the boil in a large saucepan or pot, add 1 tablespoon of salt and drop in the pasta all at once, stirring until the strands are submerged.
4 When the pasta is cooked *al dente*, return the pan with the sauce to a low heat, drain the pasta and add it to the pan. Toss over the heat until the pasta is well coated. Serve at once, grinding some fresh black pepper over each serving.

Also good with: *spaghettini, penne*

FETTUCCE
Ribbons

TAGLIOLINI ALLA ROMAGNOLA

Tagliolini with Prosciutto

This is a classic example of how simple good Italian food can be. Handmade egg noodles, good quality prosciutto, parmigiano-reggiano and butter are all you need to make this wonderful dish. The only possible improvement would be the addition of fresh early peas.

INGREDIENTS

For *tagliolini* made with 3 eggs (see page 36)
or 500g (1lb) dried, shop-bought egg *tagliolini*

150g (5oz) fresh shelled peas (optional)
90g (3oz) butter
125g (4oz) prosciutto, *cut from a 6mm (¼in) thick slice into thin strips*
60g (2oz) freshly grated parmigiano-reggiano *cheese*

PREPARATION

1 If using peas, cook them in boiling salted water until tender. Drain and set aside.
2 Pour 4 litres (7 pints) of water into a large saucepan or pot and place over a high heat.
3 Melt the butter in a large sauté pan over a medium-high heat. Add the *prosciutto* and sauté until it is lightly browned: 2–3 minutes. If using peas, add them now and sauté for 5 more minutes. Remove from the heat and set aside.
4 When the water for the pasta is boiling, and the sauce is off the heat, add 1 tablespoon of salt to the boiling water and drop in the pasta all at once, stirring well.
5 When the pasta is cooked *al dente*, drain and toss with the sauce, adding the grated cheese. Serve at once.

Also good with: *fettuccine, tagliatelle*

FETTUCCINE ALLE ERBE E PANNA ROSA

Fettuccine with Herbs, Fresh Tomatoes and Cream

You need fresh herbs and the best-quality ripe plum tomatoes you can find for this recipe.

INGREDIENTS

For *fettuccine* made with 3 eggs (see page 36)
or 500g (1lb) dried, shop-bought egg *fettuccine*

60g (2oz) butter
2 tsps finely chopped fresh basil
1 tsp finely chopped fresh rosemary
1 tsp finely chopped fresh sage
½ beef bouillon cube
1kg (2lb) fresh ripe plum tomatoes, peeled, seeded and cut into 6mm (¼in) dice
salt and freshly ground black pepper
120ml (8 tbsps) double cream

PREPARATION

1 Pour 4 litres (7 pints) of water into a large saucepan or pot and place over a high heat.
2 Melt the butter in a large sauté pan over a medium heat. Add all the herbs and the bouillon cube and stir with a wooden spoon, until the cube has dissolved completely: about 1 minute. Be careful not to let the butter burn.
3 Add the tomatoes, season with salt and black pepper and cook until they have reduced and separated from the butter: 5–10 minutes.
4 Raise the heat to medium-high and pour in the cream. Cook, stirring frequently, until it has reduced by about half, then remove the pan from the heat and set aside.
5 When the water for the pasta is boiling, and the sauce is off the heat, add 1 tablespoon of salt to the boiling water and drop in the pasta all at once, stirring well.
6 When the pasta is cooked *al dente*, drain and toss with the sauce. Serve at once.

Also good with: *tagliatelle* (*spaghetti* is acceptable but only as a last resort)

FETTUCCINE ALLE ZUCCHINE E ZAFFERANO

Fettuccine with Courgettes and Saffron Cream

In this elegant sauce the cream takes on the flavour of the saffron and courgettes. It is perfectly suited to homemade egg pasta.

INGREDIENTS

**For *fettuccine* made with 3 eggs (see page 36)
or 500g (1lb) dried, shop-bought egg *fettuccine***

60g (2oz) butter
100g (3½oz) finely chopped onion
*700g (1½ lb) courgettes, cut into sticks 4cm (1½in) long
and 6mm (¼in) thick*
salt and freshly ground black pepper
250ml (8fl oz) double cream
¼ tsp finely chopped saffron strands
6 tbsps freshly grated parmigiano-reggiano cheese

PREPARATION

1 Pour 4 litres (7 pints) of water into a large saucepan or pot and place over a high heat.
2 Melt the butter in a large sauté pan over a medium heat. Add the onion and cook until it has has softened and turned a rich golden colour.
3 Raise the heat to medium-high and add the courgettes. Cook until they are tender and lightly browned. Season with salt and black pepper.
4 Pour in the cream and sprinkle on the saffron. Cook, stirring frequently, until the cream has reduced by half. Remove from the heat.
5 When the water for the pasta is boiling, and the sauce is off the heat, add 1 tablespoon of salt to the boiling water and drop in the pasta all at once, stirring well.
6 When the pasta is cooked *al dente*, drain and toss with the sauce, adding the grated cheese. Serve at once.

Also good with: *tagliatelle*

Fettuccine al Tonno e Panna allo Zafferano

Fettuccine with Fresh Tuna and Saffron Cream

Fresh tuna dries out very quickly if overcooked. Sear it briefly before adding the cream to keep it moist.

INGREDIENTS

For *fettuccine* made with 3 eggs (see page 36) or 500g (1lb) dried, shop-bought egg *fettuccine*

30g (1oz) butter
½ tsp finely chopped garlic
250g (8oz) fresh tuna, cut into 1cm (½in) chunks
salt and freshly ground black pepper
250ml (8fl oz) double cream
¼ tsp finely chopped saffron strands
1 tbsp finely chopped flat-leaf parsley

PREPARATION

1 Pour 4 litres (7 pints) of water into a large saucepan or pot and place over a high heat.
2 Melt the butter in a large sauté pan over a medium-high heat. Add the garlic and cook until it begins to sizzle.
3 Stir in the tuna and cook until it loses its raw colour: about 2 minutes. Season with salt and black pepper.
4 Pour in the cream and sprinkle on the saffron. Cook, stirring frequently, until the cream has reduced by half, then stir in the parsley and remove the pan from the heat.
5 When the water for the pasta is boiling, and the sauce is off the heat, add 1 tablespoon of salt to the boiling water and drop in the pasta all at once, stirring well.
6 When the pasta is cooked *al dente*, return the sauce to a low heat, drain the pasta and toss it with the sauce. Serve at once.

Also good with: *tagliatelle*

Fettuccine alle Verdure

Fettuccine with Vegetables and Roasted Red Pepper Sauce

This is a great dish for health-conscious vegetarians. Instead of cream I use a purée of roasted red peppers to bind the ingredients together.

INGREDIENTS

For *fettuccine* made with 3 eggs (see page 36) or 500g (1lb) dried, shop-bought egg *fettuccine*

2 red peppers
30g (1oz) butter, softened to room temperature
salt and freshly ground black pepper
60ml (4 tbsps) extra-virgin olive oil
1 tsp finely chopped garlic
1 large aubergine, peeled and cut into 1cm (½in) dice
350g (12oz) courgettes, cut into 1cm (½in) dice
1 yellow pepper, cored and seeded, peeled, and cut into 1cm (½in) squares
4 tbsps freshly grated parmigiano-reggiano cheese

PREPARATION

1 Roast the red peppers under the grill or over an open flame until the skin is charred on all sides. Place them in a bowl and cover the bowl tightly with cling film. After about 20 minutes take the peppers out, cut them in half, remove the core and scrape away the blistered skin and the seeds. Place the peppers in a food processor with the butter, season with salt and black pepper, and grind until creamy. Remove and set aside.
2 Pour 4 litres (7 pints) of water into a large saucepan or pot and place over a high heat.
3 Put the olive oil and the garlic in a large sauté pan over a medium heat and cook until the garlic begins to sizzle.
4 Add the aubergine, courgettes and yellow pepper and stir until well coated (do not worry if the aubergine soaks up all the oil, it will release it once it is cooked). Cover the pan and cook until the vegetables are tender: 10–15 minutes.
5 Stir the red pepper sauce into the vegetables. Remove from the heat and set aside.
6 When the water for the pasta is boiling, and the sauce is off the heat, add 1 tablespoon of salt to the boiling water and drop in the pasta all at once, stirring well.
7 When the pasta is cooked *al dente*, drain and toss with the sauce, adding the grated cheese. Serve at once.

Also good with: *tagliatelle*

FETTUCCINE COI FICHI SECCHI

Fettuccine with Dried Figs

This is definitely a recipe for the adventurous. I would not recommend serving it as a main meal, but rather as a starter, before roast duck for example. In Rome a small dish of spaghetti with oil and garlic is sometimes served at the end of the meal — fettuccine with figs would also make the perfect ending, served to 6 – 8 people.

INGREDIENTS

For *fettuccine* made with 3 eggs (see page 36) or 500g (1lb) dried, shop-bought egg *fettuccine*

175g (6oz) dried figs
60g (2oz) butter
15ml (1 tbsp) grappa or brandy
250ml (8fl oz) double cream
salt and freshly ground black pepper
6 tbsps freshly grated parmigiano-reggiano cheese

PREPARATION

1 Place the figs in a bowl, cover with lukewarm water and leave to soak for at least 30 minutes. Drain, reserving the soaking water, and cut the figs into pieces about 3 – 6mm (⅛ – ¼in) in size.
2 Pour 4 litres (7 pints) of water into a large saucepan or pot and place over a high heat.
3 Melt the butter in a sauté pan over a medium-high heat. Add the figs and cook for 1 – 2 minutes.
4 Pour in the *grappa* or brandy and let the alcohol bubble away (this will take around 1 minute). Add about 60ml (4 tbsps) of the soaking water from the figs and cook until it has evaporated.
5 Add the cream, season generously with salt and black pepper, and cook, stirring frequently, until the cream has reduced by half. Remove from the heat and set aside.
6 When the water for the pasta is boiling, and the sauce is off the heat, add 1 tablespoon of salt to the boiling water and drop in the pasta all at once, stirring well.
7 When the pasta is cooked *al dente*, drain and toss with the sauce, adding the grated cheese. Serve at once.

FETTUCCINE AL GORGONZOLA

Fettuccine with Gorgonzola Cheese

This is the classic gorgonzola sauce found in northern Italy. The gorgonzola required is dolce, the creamy, almost runny kind as opposed to the drier, sharper one. For an interesting variation, try tossing in a couple of tablespoons of toasted pine nuts at the end.

INGREDIENTS

For *fettuccine* made with 3 eggs (see page 36) or 500g (1lb) dried, shop-bought egg *fettuccine*

125g (4oz) Italian gorgonzola dolce (see introductory note above)
120ml (8 tbsps) full-cream milk
30g (1oz) butter
salt
90ml (6 tbsps) double cream
6 tbsps freshly grated parmigiano-reggiano cheese

PREPARATION

1 Pour 4 litres (7 pints) of water into a large saucepan or pot and place over a high heat.
2 Put the *gorgonzola*, milk, butter and a pinch of salt in a large sauté pan over a low heat. Cook, breaking up the cheese with a wooden spoon until it has melted completely and formed a thick creamy sauce.
3 Pour in the cream and raise the heat to medium-high. Cook, stirring frequently, until the cream has reduced to two-thirds of its original volume (this will take 3 – 5 minutes). Remove from the heat and set aside.
4 When the water for the pasta is boiling, and the sauce is off the heat, add 1 tablespoon of salt to the boiling water and drop in the pasta all at once, stirring well.
5 When the pasta is cooked *al dente*, drain and transfer to the pan with the sauce. Turn the heat on to low and toss the pasta over the heat with the sauce and the grated cheese for about 30 seconds. Serve at once.

Also good with: *spaghettini, spaghetti, garganelli, penne*

FETTUCCINE ALL'ARANCIO

Fettuccine with Orange and Mint

The idea for this came from Lori Vorst, a very good cook I've worked with. It is unusual but simple and refreshing.

INGREDIENTS

**For *fettuccine* made with 3 eggs (see page 36)
or 500g (1lb) dried, shop-bought egg *fettuccine***

90g (3oz) butter
2 tsps finely chopped orange zest
1 tsp finely shredded fresh mint
salt and freshly ground black pepper
120ml (8 tbsps) freshly squeezed orange juice
60g (2oz) freshly grated parmigiano-reggiano *cheese*

PREPARATION

1 Pour 4 litres (7 pints) of water into a large saucepan or pot and place over a high heat.
2 Melt the butter in a large sauté pan over a medium-high heat. Stir in the orange zest and mint and season with salt and black pepper.
3 Pour in the orange juice and cook until it has reduced to about two-thirds of its volume and has thickened slightly. Remove from the heat.
4 When the water for the pasta is boiling, and the sauce is off the heat, add 1 tablespoon of salt to the boiling water and drop in the pasta all at once, stirring well.
5 When the pasta is cooked *al dente*, drain and toss with the sauce, adding the grated cheese. Serve at once.

FETTUCCINE AL TARTUFO BIANCO

Fettuccine with White Truffles

If I were condemned to death and had to choose a last meal before my execution, it would be this dish, made with hand-rolled fettuccine and generous shavings of Italian white truffles.

INGREDIENTS

**For *fettuccine* made with 3 eggs (see page 36),
preferably hand-rolled**

90g (3oz) butter, cut into cubes
4 tbsps freshly grated parmigiano-reggiano *cheese*
60g (2oz), at least, of fresh white truffles

PREPARATION

1 Bring 4 litres (7 pints) of water to the boil in a large saucepan or pot, add 1½ tablespoons of salt and drop in the pasta all at once, stirring well.
2 When the pasta is cooked *al dente*, drain and place in a heated serving platter with the butter and the freshly grated cheese. Toss well and serve at once, shaving the truffles as thinly as possible over each plate using a peeler or, if you have one, a truffle shaver.

Also good with: *tagliatelle*

**Fettuccine
all'arancio**

Fettuccine al Prosciutto e Asparagi

Fettuccine with Prosciutto, Asparagus and Cream

INGREDIENTS

For *fettuccine* made with 3 eggs (see page 36)
or 500g (1lb) dried, shop-bought egg *fettuccine*

250g (8oz) asparagus
salt
45g (1½oz) butter
100g (3½oz) finely chopped onion
125g (4oz) prosciutto, cut from a 3mm (⅛in) thick slice
into thin strips
250ml (8fl oz) double cream
60g (2oz) freshly grated parmigiano-reggiano cheese

PREPARATION

1 Trim and peel the lower green portions of the asparagus. Cook whole in salted boiling water in a sauté pan until tender.

2 Reserve 120ml (8 tbsps) of the water, and cut the asparagus, when cool enough to handle, into 2cm (¾in) lengths.

3 Pour 4 litres (7 pints) of water into a large saucepan or pot and place over a high heat.

4 Melt the butter in a sauté pan over a medium heat. Add the onion and cook until it softens and turns a rich golden colour. Stir in the *prosciutto* and sauté until it has lost its raw colour.

5 Add the asparagus, raise the heat to medium-high and cook until it is lightly coloured. Pour the reserved water in and cook until it has evaporated.

6 Stir in the cream and cook until it has reduced by half. Remove from the heat and set aside.

7 When the water for the pasta is boiling, and the sauce is off the heat, add 1 tablespoon of salt to the boiling water and drop in the pasta all at once, stirring well.

8 When the pasta is cooked *al dente*, drain and toss with the sauce, adding the grated cheese. Serve at once.

Also good with: *penne, fusilli corti, garganelli*

FETTUCCINE AL LIMONE

Fettuccine with Lemon

This is a dish you have to taste to believe. When my mother wrote this recipe for her third book, she could not have dreamt how many people would become fans of it. This recipe is like the original, with minor adjustments.

INGREDIENTS

For *fettuccine* made with 3 eggs (see page 36) or 500g (1lb) dried, shop-bought egg *fettuccine*

45g (1½oz) butter
30ml (2 tbsps) freshly squeezed lemon juice
1 tsp finely chopped lemon zest
250ml (8fl oz) double cream
salt and freshly ground black pepper
60g (2oz) freshly grated parmigiano-reggiano cheese

PREPARATION

1 Pour 4 litres (7 pints) of water into a large saucepan or pot and place over a high heat.
2 Put the butter, lemon juice and zest in a large sauté pan over a medium-high heat. Once the butter has melted, let the lemon and butter bubble for about 30 seconds.
3 Pour in the cream. Season with salt and black pepper and cook, stirring frequently, until the cream has reduced by half. Remove from the heat and set aside.
4 When the water for the pasta is boiling, and the sauce is off the heat, add 1 tablespoon of salt to the boiling water and drop in the pasta all at once, stirring well.
5 When the pasta is cooked *al dente*, drain and transfer to the pan with the sauce. Turn the heat on to medium and toss the pasta over the heat with the sauce and the grated cheese for about 15 seconds. Serve at once.

TRENETTE AL PESTO DI NOCI

Trenette with Walnut Pesto

Walnut pesto, like basil pesto, is a speciality of Liguria on the Italian Riviera. It is good with fettuccine (known as trenette in Liguria) and is also traditionally served with pansoti, a triangular pasta parcel filled with five different local wild greens.

INGREDIENTS

For *trenette* (*fettuccine*) made with 3 eggs (see page 36) or 500g (1lb) dried, shop-bought egg *fettuccine*

250g (8oz) shelled walnuts
1 tsp finely chopped garlic
30ml (2 tbsps) extra-virgin olive oil
60g (2oz) full-cream ricotta
salt
60ml (4 tbsps) double cream
4 tbsps freshly grated parmigiano-reggiano cheese

PREPARATION

1 Pour 4 litres (7 pints) of water into a large saucepan or pot and place over a high heat.
2 Put the walnuts and garlic in a food processor or blender and chop as finely as possible. Pour in the olive oil and process until well mixed. Add the *ricotta*, season with salt, and process once again.
3 Transfer the mixture to a serving bowl and add the cream, mixing well with a wooden spoon.
4 When the water for the pasta is boiling, add 1 tablespoon of salt and drop in the pasta all at once, stirring well.
5 When the pasta is cooked *al dente*, put 30ml (2 tbsps) of the boiling water in the serving bowl with the walnut sauce, then drain the pasta. Toss the pasta in the serving bowl with the sauce, adding the grated cheese. Serve at once.

Also good with: *pansoti* (see introductory note above), *spaghetti*

I Pizzoccheri della Valtellina

*Buckwheat Noodles with Fontina and
Swiss Chard*

Pizzoccheri *are buckwheat noodles, a speciality of the
Valtellina region in northern Italy. You can find them
sold dried in packets in specialist food stores.*

INGREDIENTS

60g (2oz) butter
4 cloves garlic, lightly crushed and peeled but kept whole
3 – 4 fresh sage leaves
500g (1lb) pizzoccheri
*250g (8oz) new potatoes, peeled and cut
into slices 6mm (¼in) thick*
salt
*60g (2oz) Swiss chard stalks cut into sticks 2.5cm (1in)
long and 1cm (½in) wide* **and** *30g (1oz) Swiss chard
leaves torn into small pieces,* **or** *(if chard is unavailable)
60g (2oz) spinach, torn into small pieces*
125g (4oz) Italian fontina *cheese, cut into thin slivers*
60g (2oz) freshly grated parmigiano-reggiano *cheese*

PREPARATION

1 Preheat the oven to 200°C/400°F/gas 6.
2 Melt the butter in a small saucepan over a
medium-high heat. Add the garlic and the sage and
cook until the garlic has lightly browned on all
sides. Remove the pan from the heat and set aside.
3 Bring 4 litres (7 pints) of water to the boil in a
large saucepan or pot. Add 1 tablespoon of salt,
the pasta and the potatoes and cook for 8 minutes.
If using Swiss chard stalks, add them once the
pasta and potatoes have cooked for 5 minutes.
4 Drop in the Swiss chard or spinach leaves and,
when the water returns to the boil, cook for about
1 minute. The pasta should by now be *al dente*.
5 Drain the pasta and vegetables and transfer to a
mixing bowl. Pour the butter through a strainer
over them and add three-quarters of the *fontina*
and half the grated cheese. Toss well and transfer
to a buttered baking dish. Sprinkle the remaining
cheeses on top.
6 Bake on the upper shelf of the oven for about
5 minutes. Remove and allow to rest for
2 – 3 minutes before serving.

TAGLIATELLE COI GAMBERI E ASPARAGI

Tagliatelle with Prawns and Asparagus

INGREDIENTS

**For *tagliatelle* made with 3 eggs (see page 36)
or 500g (1lb) dried, shop-bought egg *tagliatelle***

*350g (12oz) asparagus
60ml (4 tbsps) extra-virgin olive oil
1 tbsp finely chopped garlic
350g (12oz) medium-sized raw prawns, peeled, deveined
if necessary, and cut into 1cm (½in) pieces
salt and freshly ground black pepper
30g (1oz) butter, at room temperature*

PREPARATION

1 Trim and peel the lower green portions of the asparagus. Cook whole in salted boiling water in a sauté pan until tender. Reserve the cooking water, and cut the asparagus, when cool enough to handle, into 2.5cm (1in) lengths.
2 Pour 4 litres (7 pints) of water into a large saucepan or pot and place over a high heat.
3 Put the olive oil and garlic in a large sauté pan over a medium-high heat and cook until the garlic begins to sizzle.
4 Add the asparagus and cook, stirring frequently, for 2–3 minutes, or less if the garlic starts to brown. Pour in 120ml (8 tbsps) of the asparagus water and cook until it has reduced by half.
5 Stir in the prawns, season generously with black pepper and cook until they have all turned pink: 2–3 minutes. The sauce should be slightly runny: if necessary add a little more asparagus water. Taste for salt and remove from the heat.
6 When the water for the pasta is boiling, add 1 tablespoon of salt and drop in the pasta all at once, stirring well.
7 When the pasta is cooked *al dente*, drain and toss thoroughly with the sauce and the butter. Serve at once.

TAGLIATELLE COI CECI

Tagliatelle with Chickpeas and Tomatoes

INGREDIENTS

**For *tagliatelle* made with 3 eggs (see page 36)
or 500g (1lb) dried, shop-bought egg *tagliatelle***

*90ml (6 tbsps) extra-virgin olive oil
100g (3½oz) finely chopped onion
1 tsp finely chopped garlic
250g (8oz) tinned whole peeled tomatoes, with their
juice, coarsely chopped
1 tsp fresh rosemary or ½tsp dried, finely chopped
salt and freshly ground black pepper
250g (8oz) drained tinned chickpeas
4 tbsps freshly grated parmigiano-reggiano cheese*

PREPARATION

1 Put the olive oil and onion in a large sauté pan over a medium heat and cook until the onion softens and turns a rich golden colour.
2 Add the garlic and continue cooking until it begins to change colour.
3 Add the tomatoes and rosemary, season with salt and black pepper and cook until the tomatoes have reduced and separated from the oil: about 10–20 minutes.
4 Pour 4 litres (7 pints) of water into a large saucepan or pot and place over a high heat.
5 Add the chickpeas to the sauce in the sauté pan and cook for another 5 minutes. Using a slotted spoon, take out about half of the chickpeas. Purée them through a food mill or mash them with a fork and return them to the pan. Cook for another minute, stirring, then remove from the heat and set aside.
6 When the water for the pasta is boiling, add 1 tablespoon of salt and drop in the pasta all at once, stirring well.
7 When the pasta is cooked *al dente*, drain and toss with the sauce, adding the grated cheese. Serve at once.

Also good with: *tonnarelli*

PAGLIA E FIENO COI PISELLI

Yellow and Green Fettuccine with Peas, Prosciutto and Cream

The yellow and green noodles for this dish are called paglia e fieno, *which means "straw and hay". In this version peas and* prosciutto *provide a contrast of sweet and savoury flavours.*

INGREDIENTS

For *paglia e fieno* made with 3 eggs (see page 36) or 500g (1lb) dried, shop-bought *paglia e fieno*

*350g (12oz) fresh shelled peas **or** a 300g (10oz) packet of frozen tiny peas, thawed*
60g (2oz) butter
4 tbsps finely chopped onion
125g (4oz) prosciutto, *cut from a 6mm (¼in) thick slice into thin strips*
salt and freshly ground black pepper
250ml (8fl oz) double cream
60g (2oz) freshly grated parmigiano-reggiano *cheese*

PREPARATION

1 If using fresh peas, cook them now in boiling salted water until tender. Drain and set aside.
2 Pour 4 litres (7 pints) of water into a large saucepan or pot and place over a high heat.
3 Melt the butter in a large sauté pan over a medium-low heat. Add the onion and cook until it has softened and turned a rich golden colour. Add the *prosciutto* and continue cooking, stirring, until it has lost its raw colour: 1–2 minutes.
4 Raise the heat to medium-high and add the cooked fresh peas or the thawed frozen ones. Season lightly with salt (remembering that the *prosciutto* is already salty) and black pepper and cook, stirring occasionally, for 2–3 minutes.
5 Pour in the cream and cook, stirring frequently, until it has reduced by half. Remove the pan from the heat and set aside.
6 When the water for the pasta is boiling, and the sauce is off the heat, add 1 tablespoon of salt to the boiling water and drop in the pasta all at once, stirring well.
7 When the pasta is cooked *al dente*, drain and toss with the sauce, adding the grated cheese. Taste for salt and serve at once.

PAGLIA E FIENO AI FUNGHI

Yellow and Green Fettuccine with Mushrooms, Ham and Cream

Paglia e fieno *is sometimes served with mushrooms instead of peas. Ham is used here because its milder flavour is better suited to mushrooms than* prosciutto *is.*

INGREDIENTS

For *paglia e fieno* made with 3 eggs (see page 36) or 500g (1lb) dried, shop-bought egg *paglia e fieno*

60g (2oz) butter
4 tbsps finely chopped onion
125g (4oz) Italian boiled ham, cut from a 6mm (¼in) thick slice into thin strips
350g (12oz) fresh white mushrooms, cleaned and cut into 1cm (½in) dice
salt and freshly ground black pepper
250ml (8fl oz) double cream
60g (2oz) freshly grated parmigiano-reggiano *cheese*

PREPARATION

1 Pour 4 litres (7 pints) of water into a large saucepan or pot and place over a high heat.
2 Melt the butter in a large sauté pan over a medium-low heat. Add the onion and cook until it has softened and turned a rich golden colour. Add the ham and continue cooking, stirring, until it is lightly coloured: 1–2 minutes.
3 Raise the heat to medium-high and add the mushrooms. Season lightly with salt (remembering that the ham is already salty) and black pepper and cook, stirring occasionally, until all the water the mushrooms give off has evaporated. Cook for a further 4–5 minutes after reaching this point.
4 Pour in the cream and cook, stirring frequently, until it has reduced by half. Remove the pan from the heat and set aside.
5 When the water for the pasta is boiling, and the sauce is off the heat, add 1 tablespoon of salt to the boiling water and drop in the pasta all at once, stirring well.
6 When the pasta is cooked *al dente*, drain and toss with the sauce, adding the grated cheese. Taste for salt and serve at once.

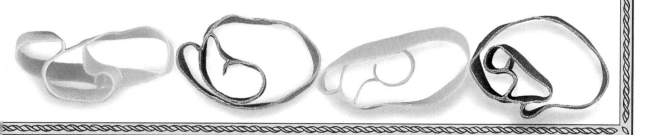

Pappardelle al coniglio
(page 103)

Tonnarelli al
radicchio e belga
(page 103)

**Paglia e fieno coi piselli
(page 99)**

PAPPARDELLE AL SUGO DI PICCIONE

Pappardelle with Squab

It was always a special treat when my mother made pan-roasted squab (young pigeon) for the family. I've adapted her recipe into a sauce for pasta.

INGREDIENTS

For *pappardelle* made with 3 eggs (see page 36) *or* 500g (1lb) dried, shop-bought egg *pappardelle*

2 squab, about 500g (1lb) each
2 thin slices of pancetta
12 fresh sage leaves, 8 finely chopped and 4 whole
45g (1½oz) butter
30ml (2 tbsps) vegetable oil
salt and freshly ground black pepper
120ml (8 tbsps) dry white wine
6 tbsps freshly grated parmigiano-reggiano cheese

PREPARATION

1 Remove the organs from the birds' cavities and save the livers. Wash the squab under cold running water and pat them dry. Put a slice of *pancetta*, the liver and 2 whole sage leaves inside each bird.
2 Put a third of the butter and all the vegetable oil in a large, deep sauté pan over a medium-high heat. Allow the butter to foam and, when it begins to subside, put in the squab and the chopped sage. Brown the birds on all sides.
3 Season with salt and black pepper, then pour in the white wine and let it bubble for about 30 seconds. Turn the heat down to medium-low and cover the pan. Cook, turning the squab every 15 minutes, until very tender: about 1 hour.
4 Remove the birds from the pan and allow them to cool. Remove all the meat from the bones and cut it into pieces no larger than 2cm (¾in). Finely chop the livers and the *pancetta*.
5 Skim any excess fat from the juices in the sauté pan and return to it the meat, livers and *pancetta*. Cook over a medium-high heat until the sauce has reduced and is no longer watery. Remove from the heat and set aside.

You can prepare the sauce ahead of time up to this point and refrigerate it.

6 Bring 4 litres (7 pints) of water to the boil in a large saucepan or pot, add 1 tablespoon of salt and drop in the pasta all at once, stirring well.
7 When the pasta is cooked *al dente*, drain and toss with the sauce, the remaining butter and the grated cheese. Serve at once.

PAPPARDELLE COI FEGATINI DI POLLO

Pappardelle with Chicken Livers

This is a classic Tuscan dish. My favourite recipe for it is my mother's, to which I have made very minor changes.

INGREDIENTS

For *pappardelle* made with 3 eggs (see page 36) *or* 500g (1lb) dried, shop-bought egg *pappardelle*

30ml (2 tbsps) extra-virgin olive oil
30g (1oz) butter
2 tbsps finely chopped shallots
½ tsp finely chopped garlic
60g (2oz) pancetta, finely diced
1 tsp chopped fresh sage *or* ½ tsp dried
125g (4oz) minced beef
250g (8oz) chicken livers, trimmed of any fat and cut into approximately 1cm (½in) pieces
salt and freshly ground black pepper
2 tsps tomato purée
60ml (4 tbsps) dry white vermouth
6 tbsps freshly grated parmigiano-reggiano cheese

PREPARATION

1 Put the olive oil, butter and shallots in a saucepan over a medium heat and sauté until the shallots begin to colour.
2 Stir in the garlic and, after about 30 seconds, the *pancetta* and sage. Cook until the *pancetta* begins to brown lightly.
3 Add the minced beef and cook, breaking it up with a wooden spoon, until it loses its raw colour.
4 Add the chicken livers, season with salt and black pepper and cook for a few more minutes until they have lost their raw colour.
5 Pour 4 litres (7 pints) of water into a large saucepan or pot and place over a high heat.
6 Dissolve the tomato purée in the vermouth. Raise the heat to medium-high under the sauce, pour in the vermouth and cook, stirring frequently, until most of the liquid has evaporated: 5–10 minutes. Remove from the heat.
7 When the water for the pasta is boiling, and the sauce is off the heat, add 1 tablespoon of salt to the boiling water and drop in the pasta all at once, stirring well.
8 When the pasta is cooked *al dente*, drain and toss with the sauce, adding the grated cheese. Serve at once.

Also good with: *tagliatelle*

PAPPARDELLE AL CONIGLIO

Pappardelle with Rabbit

Pappardelle *with hare sauce is a classic Tuscan dish. Since it can be difficult to find wild hare, I've adapted the recipe for rabbit, a milder meat.*

INGREDIENTS

For *pappardelle* made with 3 eggs (see page 36) or 500g (1lb) dried, shop-bought egg *pappardelle*

45ml (3 tbsps) extra-virgin olive oil
45g (1½oz) butter
4 tbsps finely chopped onion
4 tbsps finely diced carrot
4 tbsps finely diced celery
350g (12oz) boneless rabbit meat, cut into cubes no larger than 1cm (½in)
1 tsp finely chopped fresh rosemary or ½ tsp dried
2 tbsps juniper berries
250ml (8fl oz) dry red wine
350g (12oz) tinned whole peeled tomatoes, with their juice, coarsely chopped
salt and freshly ground black pepper
60g (2oz) freshly grated parmigiano-reggiano *cheese*

PREPARATION

1 Put the olive oil, a third of the butter and all the onion in a heavy-bottomed, deep saucepan over a medium heat and sauté until the onion has turned a light golden colour.
2 Add the carrot and celery and cook until they begin to change colour: 5–10 minutes.
3 Stir in the rabbit, rosemary and juniper berries and cook until the meat has browned lightly.
4 Turn the heat up to medium-high and pour in the red wine. After about 2 minutes, when the alcohol from the wine has bubbled away, add the tomatoes and season with salt and black pepper.
5 When the tomatoes begin to bubble, reduce the heat to low and cook until the rabbit has become very tender: at least 1 hour. If all the liquid evaporates before the rabbit is fully tender, add a little water. When done, remove from the heat.

You can prepare the sauce ahead of time up to this point and refrigerate it.

6 Bring 4 litres (7 pints) of water to the boil in a large saucepan or pot, add 1 tablespoon of salt and drop in the pasta all at once, stirring well.
7 When the pasta is cooked *al dente*, drain and toss with the sauce, the remaining butter and the grated cheese. Serve at once.

Also good with: *penne rigate, elicoidali, millerighe*

TONNARELLI AL RADICCHIO E BELGA

Tonnarelli with Radicchio and Chicory

Vegetable oil is used here to prevent the butter from burning. Olive oil is used wherever its flavour enhances the dish.

INGREDIENTS

For *tonnarelli* made with 3 eggs (see page 36) or 500g (1lb) dried, shop-bought egg *tonnarelli*

15ml (1 tbsp) vegetable oil
30g (1oz) butter
6 tbsps finely chopped onion
125g (4oz) smoked bacon, cut from a 1cm (½in) thick slice into thin strips
500g (1lb) radicchio, *shredded*
500g (1lb) chicory, shredded
salt and freshly ground black pepper
250ml (8fl oz) double cream
1 tbsp finely chopped flat-leaf parsley
60g (2oz) freshly grated parmigiano-reggiano *cheese*

PREPARATION

1 Put the vegetable oil, butter and onion in a sauté pan (large enough to hold the *radicchio* and chicory later) over a medium heat and sauté until the onion has softened and turned golden.
2 Add the bacon and cook until it is well browned but not crisp.
3 Add the *radicchio* and chicory, season with salt and black pepper and stir until the vegetables are coated with the oil and butter. Turn the heat down to low, cover the pan and cook, stirring occasionally, until the *radicchio* and chicory have wilted completely and are almost creamy in consistency: about 15–20 minutes.
4 Pour 4 litres (7 pints) of water into a large saucepan or pot and place over a high heat.
5 Uncover the sauté pan, raise the heat to medium-high and let any liquid the vegetables have given off boil away. Pour in the cream and cook, stirring frequently, until it has reduced by half. Stir in the parsley and remove from the heat.
6 When the water for the pasta is boiling, and the sauce is off the heat, add 1 tablespoon of salt to the boiling water and put in the pasta all at once, stirring well.
7 When the pasta is cooked *al dente*, return the pan with the sauce to a low heat, drain the pasta and toss with the sauce in the pan, adding the grated cheese. Serve at once.

Also good with: *spaghetti, fusilli lunghi, penne*

TONNARELLI AI GAMBERI E FUNGHI

Tonnarelli with Prawns and Mushrooms

This sauce was inspired by a pasta dish Del Pearl, one of my sous-chefs, created. Prawns and mushrooms are wonderful together, particularly with the addition of dried porcini.

INGREDIENTS

For *tonnarelli* made with 3 eggs (see page 36) or 500g (1lb) dried, shop-bought egg *tonnarelli*

30g (1oz) dried porcini
90ml (6 tbsps) extra-virgin olive oil
90g (3oz) onion, thinly sliced lengthways
350g (12oz) fresh white mushrooms, thinly sliced
salt and freshly ground black pepper
250g (8oz) fresh ripe plum tomatoes, peeled, seeded
and cut into 1cm (½in) dice
350g (12oz) medium-sized raw prawns, peeled, deveined
if necessary, and cut into thirds
120ml (8 tbsps) double cream

PREPARATION

1 Soak the dried *porcini* in a bowl with 250ml (8fl oz) lukewarm water for at least 20 minutes. Lift them out, squeezing the excess water back into the bowl, then rinse under cold running water and coarsely chop them. Filter the water they soaked in through kitchen paper or a coffee filter and set aside.

2 Put the olive oil and onion in a large sauté pan over a medium heat and cook until the onion softens and turns a rich golden colour.

3 Add the reconstituted *porcini* with their filtered water, raise the heat to medium-high and cook, stirring, until almost all the water has evaporated. Add the fresh mushrooms, season with salt and black pepper and cook, stirring, until they are tender and the water they release has evaporated.

4 Pour 4 litres (7 pints) of water into a large saucepan or pot and place over a high heat.

5 Put the tomatoes into the sauté pan and cook for 2 minutes. Stir in the prawns, add the cream and cook, stirring frequently, until the cream has reduced by half. Remove the pan from the heat.

6 When the water for the pasta is boiling, and the sauce is off the heat, add 1 tablespoon of salt to the boiling water and drop in the pasta all at once, stirring well.

7 When the pasta is cooked *al dente*, drain and toss with the sauce. Serve at once.

Also good with: *spaghetti, fusilli lunghi*

Porcini

Extra-virgin olive oil

Onion

Fresh mushrooms

Salt

Black pepper

Tonnarelli ai
gamberi e funghi

Plum tomatoes

Prawns

Double cream

Tonnarelli

Tonnarelli al Sugo di Cipolle

Tonnarelli with Onions, Anchovies and Capers

The lowly onion becomes a succulent sauce with the help of slow cooking. The anchovies are only barely detectable.

INGREDIENTS

For *tonnarelli* made with 3 eggs (see page 36) *or* 500g (1lb) dried, shop-bought egg *tonnarelli*

120ml (8 tbsps) extra-virgin olive oil
6–8 anchovy fillets, chopped
700g (1½lb) onions, finely chopped
salt and freshly ground black pepper
60ml (4 tbsps) dry white wine
3 tbsps capers
2 tbsps finely chopped parsley

PREPARATION

1 Put the olive oil and anchovies in a large sauté pan over a medium-low heat and stir with a wooden spoon until the anchovies have dissolved.
2 Add the onions, season lightly with salt and with black pepper and cook until the onions soften and become very tender: about 20–30 minutes.
3 Pour 4 litres (7 pints) of water into a large saucepan or pot and place over a high heat.
4 Raise the heat under the sauté pan to medium-high and cook, stirring, until the onions become a rich, golden colour.
5 Pour in the wine and cook until most of it has evaporated. Add the capers and parsley and cook for 2 more minutes. Remove from the heat.
6 When the water for the pasta is boiling, and the sauce is off the heat, add 1 tablespoon of salt to the boiling water and drop in the pasta all at once, stirring well.
7 When the pasta is cooked *al dente*, drain and toss with the sauce. Serve at once.

Also good with: *spaghetti, spaghettini, fusilli lunghi*

Tonnarelli al Melone

Tonnarelli with Cantaloupe Melon

Although pasta with melon may sound an unlikely combination, I think you'll find the result surprisingly good. This is a recipe my parents and I discovered at a restaurant in Venice owned by a talented, creative and very young chef called Silvano. What follows is a variation of my mother's recipe, which she based on the recipe Silvano gave her.

INGREDIENTS

For *tonnarelli* made with 3 eggs (see page 36) *or* 500g (1lb) dried, shop-bought egg *tonnarelli*

60g (2oz) butter
1 medium-sized cantaloupe melon, rind and seeds removed and flesh cut into 6mm (¼in) dice
salt and freshly ground black pepper
15ml (1 tbsp) freshly squeezed lemon juice
1 tsp tomato purée
250ml (8fl oz) double cream
60g (2oz) freshly grated parmigiano-reggiano *cheese*

PREPARATION

1 Pour 4 litres (7 pints) of water into a large saucepan or pot and place over a high heat.
2 Melt the butter in a large sauté pan over a medium-high heat. When the butter foam subsides, stir in the melon, coating it well, and cook, stirring occasionally, until almost all the liquid it releases has evaporated.
3 Season generously with salt and black pepper and add the lemon juice and tomato purée. Pour in the cream and cook, stirring frequently, until it has reduced by half. Remove from the heat.
4 When the water for the pasta is boiling, and the sauce is off the heat, add 1 tablespoon of salt to the boiling water and drop in the pasta all at once, stirring well.
5 When the pasta is cooked *al dente*, drain and toss with the sauce, adding the grated cheese. Serve at once.

Also good with: *spaghetti* (but reduce the cream to 180ml/6fl oz)

TONNARELLI AL GRANCHIO E RUCOLA

Tonnarelli with Crab and Rocket

This is a recipe I found in Positano in southern Italy, which I tried at home with great success using Dungeness crab, native to the Pacific coast of the US. Other types of crab, if meaty and sweet-tasting, will work well too.

INGREDIENTS

For *tonnarelli* made with 3 eggs (see page 36) or 500g (1lb) dried, shop-bought egg *tonnarelli*

120ml (8 tbsps) extra-virgin olive oil
1 tsp finely chopped garlic
¼ tsp (or more) crushed chillies
500g (1lb) fresh ripe plum tomatoes, peeled, seeded and cut into 1cm (½in) dice
125g (4oz) rocket, washed, long stems removed, and coarsely shredded
salt
250g (8oz) cooked crab meat

PREPARATION

1 Pour 4 litres (7 pints) of water into a large saucepan or pot and place over a high heat.
2 Put the olive oil, garlic and crushed chillies in a large sauté pan over a medium-high heat and cook until the garlic begins to change colour.
3 Add the tomatoes and cook for about 5 minutes until they begin to break down and the oil takes on a reddish colour. This should happen quickly and the tomatoes should not go through the usual process of releasing water and cooking down until they have reduced. You may need to turn the heat up even higher but take care not to burn them.
4 Add the rocket, season with salt and add about 30ml (2 tbsps) of water. Cook until the rocket has wilted completely: 2–3 minutes.
5 When the water for the pasta is boiling, add 1 tablespoon of salt and drop in the pasta all at once, stirring well.
6 Add the crab to the sauce and cook, stirring for about 1 minute. Remove from the heat.
7 When the pasta is cooked *al dente*, drain and toss with the sauce. If it appears to be too dry, drizzle with a little fresh olive oil. Serve at once.

Also good with: *spaghetti, fusilli lunghi*

TONNARELLI AI CANESTRELLI

Tonnarelli with Scallops

This is one of my favourites of my mother's recipes, and this version has only slight variations from hers. Its preparation takes very little time and is a perfect example of the simple and direct Italian approach to bringing out the flavour of the main ingredient. The breadcrumbs add texture and absorb some of the olive oil to help it cling to the pasta.

INGREDIENTS

For *tonnarelli* made with 3 eggs (see page 36) or 500g (1lb) dried, shop-bought egg *tonnarelli*

150ml (10 tbsps) extra-virgin olive oil
2 tsps finely chopped garlic
¼ tsp (or more) crushed chillies
2 tbsps finely chopped flat-leaf parsley
500g (1lb) small scallops, without shells or coral, of which 125g (4oz) are finely chopped
salt
4 tbsps plain breadcrumbs, toasted

PREPARATION

1 Pour 4 litres (7 pints) of water into a large saucepan or pot and place over a high heat.
2 Put all but 30ml (2 tbsps) of the olive oil and all the garlic and crushed chillies in a sauté pan over a medium-high heat and cook until the garlic begins to change colour.
3 Add the parsley and stir well. Add the whole scallops, season with salt and cook, stirring, until they are no longer translucent: 3–5 minutes. Add the chopped scallops and cook, stirring, for another minute. Remove from the heat.
4 When the water for the pasta is boiling, and the sauce is off the heat, add 1 tablespoon of salt to the boiling water and drop in the pasta all at once, stirring well.
5 When the pasta is cooked *al dente*, drain and toss with the sauce, the toasted breadcrumbs and the remaining olive oil. Taste for salt and spiciness and serve at once.

Also good with: *spaghettini, spaghetti* (but for each one use only 90ml (6 tbsps) of olive oil in step 2)

TUBI
Tubes

PENNE AL CAVOLFIORE E PANNA

Penne with Cauliflower, Tomatoes and Cream

INGREDIENTS

For 500g (1lb) *penne*

350g (12oz) cauliflower, leaves and stem removed
60g (2oz) butter
60g (2oz) finely chopped onion
¼ tsp crushed chillies
salt
*500g (1lb) fresh ripe plum tomatoes, peeled, seeded
and cut into 1cm (½in) dice*
180ml (6fl oz) double cream
60g (2oz) freshly grated parmigiano-reggiano *cheese*

PREPARATION

1 Cook the cauliflower in abundant unsalted boiling water until tender. When cool enough to handle, cut it into 2cm (¾in) pieces.
2 Pour 4 litres (7 pints) of water into a large saucepan or pot and place over a high heat.
3 Melt the butter in a large sauté pan over a medium heat. Add the onion and cook until it has softened and turned a rich golden colour.
4 Add the crushed chillies and the cauliflower and season generously with salt. Sauté until the cauliflower is lightly browned: 8 – 10 minutes. Stir in the tomatoes and cook for 1 minute.
5 When the water for the pasta is boiling, add 1 tablespoon of salt and drop in the pasta all at once, stirring well.
6 Pour the cream into the pan with the sauce and cook until the cream has reduced by about half.
7 When the pasta is cooked *al dente*, drain and toss with the sauce, adding the grated cheese. Taste for salt and serve at once.

Also good with: *orecchiette, fusilli corti, gnocchi, lumache*

DENTI D'ELEFANTE AI PEPERONI E BIETE

Denti d'Elefante with Peppers and Swiss Chard

INGREDIENTS

For 500g (1lb) *denti d'elefante*

45ml (3 tbsps) extra-virgin olive oil
4 cloves garlic, lightly crushed and peeled but kept whole
2 red peppers, cored and seeded, peeled,
  and cut into 2cm (¾in) squares
*250g (8oz) Swiss chard **or** (if chard is unavailable)*
  spinach leaves, roughly chopped
salt and freshly ground black pepper
30g (1oz) butter
30ml (2 tbsps) balsamic vinegar
6 tbsps freshly grated parmigiano-reggiano *cheese*

PREPARATION

1 Put the olive oil and garlic in a large sauté pan over a high heat and cook until the garlic cloves have browned on all sides.
2 Discard the garlic. Add the peppers and cook, stirring often, until they are lightly browned.
3 Reduce the heat to medium and add the chard or spinach and 30ml (2 tbsps) of water. Season with salt and black pepper and cook until the vegetables are tender. Remove from the heat.
4 Meanwhile, bring 4 litres (7 pints) of water to the boil in a large saucepan or pot, add 1 tablespoon of salt and drop in the pasta all at once, stirring well.
5 When the pasta is almost done, return the pan with the sauce to a low heat and swirl in the butter. Once the pasta is cooked *al dente*, drain and toss with the sauce in the pan, adding the balsamic vinegar and the grated cheese. Serve at once.

Also good with: *fusilli corti, penne*

CAVATAPPI ALLA BOSCAIOLA

Cavatappi with Wild Mushrooms and Tomatoes

Boscaiola *means "woodsman style" and this dish will evoke sensations of strolling through woods in autumn. If you have fresh* porcini (Boletus edulis), *use them instead of the white mushrooms, and disregard steps 1 and 3. In the absence of fresh* porcini, *dried* porcini *will endow cultivated mushrooms with the flavour of wild ones.*

INGREDIENTS

For 500g (1lb) *cavatappi*

30g (1oz) dried porcini
60ml (4 tbsps) extra-virgin olive oil
1 tsp finely chopped garlic
1 tbsp finely chopped flat-leaf parsley
350g (12oz) fresh white mushrooms,
cut into 1cm (½in) dice
250g (8oz) tinned whole peeled tomatoes, with their juice, coarsely chopped
salt and freshly ground black pepper
30g (1oz) butter
6 tbsps freshly grated parmigiano-reggiano *cheese*

Flat-leaf parsley

PREPARATION

1 Soak the dried *porcini* in a bowl with 250ml (8fl oz) lukewarm water for at least 20 minutes. Lift them out, squeezing the excess water back into the bowl, then rinse under cold running water and coarsely chop them. Filter the water they soaked in through kitchen paper or a coffee filter and set aside.

2 Put the olive oil and garlic in a large sauté pan over a medium-high heat and cook until the garlic begins to change colour, then stir in the parsley.

3 Add the reconstituted *porcini* with their filtered water and cook until the water has evaporated.

4 Put in the fresh mushrooms and cook until all the water they release has evaporated.

5 Pour in the tomatoes, season with salt and black pepper and cook until the tomatoes have reduced and separated from the oil. Remove from the heat.

You can prepare the sauce ahead of time up to this point and refrigerate it.

6 Bring 4 litres (7 pints) of water to the boil in a large saucepan or pot, add 1 tablespoon of salt and drop in the pasta all at once, stirring well.

7 When the pasta is almost done, return the sauce to a medium-low heat. Once the pasta is cooked *al dente*, drain and toss with the sauce, adding the butter and the grated cheese. Serve at once.

Also good with: *maccheroni, fusilli lunghi, penne*

Garlic

Extra-virgin olive oil

Dried porcini

Fresh
mushrooms

Tinned
tomatoes

Salt

*Black
pepper*

Butter

*Parmigiano-
reggiano*

Cavatappi

**Cavatappi
alla boscaiola**

ELICOIDALI AL POLLO

Elicoidali with Braised Chicken and Tomatoes

I have never been particularly fond of chicken with pasta because I have always found the chicken too bland in flavour and texture. However, customers often request a chicken sauce. I wanted to create a good one, and I discussed my dilemma with my mother. She suggested braising a chicken with tomatoes, then removing the meat from the bone and returning it to cook in the tomato and its own juices until it became a sauce. I tried it and, with the addition of a small amount of crushed chillies, came up with a dish that proved successful and popular.

INGREDIENTS

For 500g (1lb) *elicoidali*

45g (1½oz) butter
30ml (2 tbsps) vegetable oil
6 cloves garlic, lightly crushed and peeled but kept whole
2 sprigs fresh rosemary or 1 tsp finely chopped dried
1kg (2lb) chicken legs, thighs and wings
120ml (4fl oz) dry white wine
500g (1lb) tinned whole peeled tomatoes, with their juice, coarsely chopped
¼ tsp crushed chillies
salt
6 tbsps freshly grated parmigiano-reggiano *cheese*

PREPARATION

1 Put 15g (½oz) of the butter and all the vegetable oil, garlic and rosemary in a casserole (large enough to take the chicken pieces without too much overlap) over a medium-high heat. Cook until the garlic cloves have browned nicely.
2 Discard the garlic. Put in the chicken pieces, skin-side down. Brown on all sides (this will be easier if you do not crowd the pan so, if necessary, cook the chicken in two batches), transferring to a warmed plate when done.
3 Discard the rosemary (if using fresh sprigs) and return all the chicken to the pan. Raise the heat to high, pour in the white wine and let it bubble for about 1 minute so that the alcohol evaporates.

4 Add the tomatoes and the crushed chillies and season with salt. When the tomatoes start to bubble, turn the heat down to low and cover the pan with the lid on loosely so that it leaves a gap. Cook, turning the chicken occasionally and adding some water if more liquid is needed, until the meat is very tender and almost falls off the bone: 45 minutes to an hour. Cooking it a little longer will not hurt, nor should you worry if there seems to be a lot of liquid left over at the end.
5 Take out the chicken pieces and allow them to cool. When cool enough to handle, remove the meat from the bone in small pieces, discarding the fat and skin. Skim off the fat from the sauce and return the meat to it.

You can prepare the sauce ahead of time up to this point and refrigerate it.

6 Bring 4 litres (7 pints) of water to the boil in a large saucepan or pot, add 1 tablespoon of salt and drop in the pasta all at once, stirring well.
7 Reheat the sauce over a medium-low heat. If the sauce was prepared ahead of time, the chicken may have absorbed all the liquid and become too dry. You can add a little chicken broth or water to moisten it. If, however, there is too much liquid, simply raise the heat and let it reduce down.
8 When the pasta is cooked *al dente*, drain and toss with the sauce, the remaining butter and the grated cheese. Taste for salt and serve at once.

Also good with: *penne, rigatoni, lumache, pappardelle*

PENNE AI QUATTRO FORMAGGI

Penne with Four Cheeses

Pasta and cheese is an inspired combination with a wide appeal and almost everyone has their favourite concoction. This is mine. The pronounced taste of the gorgonzola, *the richness of the* fontina, *the savour of the* parmigiano-reggiano *and the delicate creaminess of the* mascarpone *all complement each other perfectly, and when the dish is baked, the pasta absorbs all the flavours. Choose Italian-made cheeses.*

INGREDIENTS

For 500g (1lb) *penne*

15g (½oz) butter
120ml (4fl oz) double cream
125g (4oz) fontina, grated
60g (2oz) gorgonzola, crumbled
60g (2oz) mascarpone
6 tbsps freshly grated parmigiano-reggiano *cheese*
salt and freshly ground black pepper

PREPARATION

1 Preheat the oven to 230°C/450°F/gas 8.
2 Bring 4 litres (7 pints) of water to the boil in a large saucepan or pot, add 1 tablespoon of salt and drop in the pasta all at once, stirring well.
3 Put the butter and cream in a saucepan over a low heat. Stir until the butter has melted, then add all the cheeses, holding back 2 tablespoons of the grated *parmigiano-reggiano*. Stir constantly until the cheeses have melted into the cream, then season with salt and black pepper. Remove the pan from the heat and set aside.
4 When the pasta is *molto al dente* (about 1 minute away from being *al dente*), drain and toss with the sauce in a bowl until all the pasta is well coated.
5 Transfer to individual oven-to-table dishes, or a single ovenproof casserole large enough to accommodate the pasta to a depth of no more than 4cm (about 1½in). Sprinkle the remaining *parmigiano-reggiano* on top and bake until golden brown: about 10–15 minutes. When you take the dish out of the oven allow it to rest for 5 minutes before serving.

Fontina

Gorgonzola

Mascarpone

Parmigiano-reggiano

PASTA E FAGIOLI ASCIUTTA

Pasta with White Beans and Tomatoes

This is a dish I sampled in Naples. Asciutta refers to pasta with sauce, as opposed to soup, and this is similar to the classic pasta and bean soup except that it is prepared as a sauce. I like to serve it with cavatappi.

INGREDIENTS

For 500g (1lb) *cavatappi*

*45ml (3 tbsps) extra-virgin olive oil, plus
extra for serving
30g (1oz) butter
4 tbsps finely chopped onion
3 tbsps finely diced carrot
3 tbsps finely diced celery
125g (4oz) prosciutto, finely diced
350g (12oz) tinned whole peeled tomatoes, with
their juice, coarsely chopped
salt and freshly ground black pepper
175g (6oz) drained tinned white beans
2 tbsps finely chopped flat-leaf parsley
6 tbsps freshly grated parmigiano-reggiano cheese*

PREPARATION

1 Put the olive oil, butter and onion in a saucepan over a medium heat and sauté until the onion softens and turns a rich golden colour.

2 Stir in the carrot and celery and cook until they begin to brown lightly. Add the *prosciutto* and cook for about 2 minutes until it loses its raw colour.

3 Pour in the tomatoes, season with salt and black pepper, and cook until they have reduced and separated from the oil: about 15–20 minutes.

4 Pour 4 litres (7 pints) of water into a large saucepan or pot and place over a high heat.

5 Add the beans with 60ml (4fl oz) of water to the sauce and cook for 5 minutes. Take half of the beans out again, process them through a food mill or mash them with a fork, and return to the pan.

6 When the water for the pasta is boiling, add 1 tablespoon of salt and drop in the pasta all at once, stirring well.

7 Add the parsley to the sauce and cook for 2–3 more minutes. The sauce should be liquid enough to pour out of a spoon but thick enough to coat it. If necessary add a little more water, or cook a little longer if it is too runny.

8 When the pasta is cooked *al dente*, drain and toss with the sauce and the grated cheese. Grind fresh pepper and drizzle a tiny amount of good quality extra-virgin olive oil over each serving.

Also good with: *radiatori, lumache, conchiglie*

RIGATONI AL RAGU DI AGNELLO

Rigatoni with Lamb Ragù

A ragù is any sauce in which meat, vegetables and, usually, tomatoes are simmered together for a long time.

INGREDIENTS

For 500g (1lb) *rigatoni*

*15g (½oz) dried porcini
30ml (2 tbsps) extra-virgin olive oil
45g (1½oz) butter
4 tbsps finely chopped onion
6 tbsps finely diced carrot
6 tbsps finely diced celery
1 tsp fresh rosemary or ½ tsp dried, finely chopped
2 tsps juniper berries
350g (12oz) boneless lamb, cut into 6mm (¼in) dice
salt and freshly ground black pepper
90ml (6 tbsps) dry white wine
350g (12oz) tinned whole peeled tomatoes, with
their juice, coarsely chopped
4 tbsps freshly grated parmigiano-reggiano cheese*

PREPARATION

1 Soak the dried *porcini* in a bowl with 250ml (8fl oz) lukewarm water for at least 20 minutes. Lift them out, squeezing the excess water back into the bowl, then rinse under cold running water and coarsely chop them. Filter the water they soaked in through kitchen paper or a coffee filter and set aside.

2 Put the olive oil, 15g (½oz) of the butter and all the onion in a saucepan over a medium-low heat. When the onion has turned a rich golden colour, add the carrot, celery, rosemary and juniper berries. Continue sautéing until the vegetables are lightly browned.

3 Raise the heat to medium-high and put in the lamb. Cook, stirring, until the lamb has lost its raw colour. Season with salt and black pepper and pour in the white wine.

4 Let the wine bubble until it has reduced by half, then add the reconstituted *porcini* and their filtered water, and the tomatoes. Once the sauce has come to the boil, turn the heat down to low and cook for a minimum of 2 hours, stirring occasionally. The sauce is done when it is no longer watery and the lamb is very tender. Remove from the heat and set aside.

You can prepare the sauce ahead of time up to this point and refrigerate it.

5 Bring 4 litres (7 pints) of water to the boil in a large saucepan or pot, add 1 tablespoon of salt and drop in the pasta all at once, stirring well.
6 When the pasta is almost done, return the pan with the sauce to a medium heat. Once the pasta is cooked *al dente*, drain and toss with the sauce, adding the remaining butter and the grated cheese. Serve at once.

Also good with: *millerighe, elicoidali*

Rigatoni al ragù di agnello

SALSICCIA DI MAIALE

Homemade Pork Sausage

The most common pork sausage used in Italy is mild and not heavily spiced and is the kind best suited to the recipes in this book. I found it difficult to buy a comparable sausage outside Italy so I decided to try making my own. It is really very simple and, so long as you don't want to use sausage casings, no special equipment is needed. You can increase this recipe to make a large batch and then freeze it in single-use portions.

INGREDIENTS

500g (1lb) minced pork
1 tsp salt
1 tsp freshly ground black pepper
1 tsp fresh rosemary **or** ½ tsp dried, finely chopped
½ tsp finely chopped garlic
30ml (2 tbsps) dry white wine

PREPARATION

1 Combine all the ingredients in a bowl and mix thoroughly with your hands.
2 Wrap in cling film and refrigerate overnight before using or freezing.

PENNE AI RAPINI E SALSICCIA

Penne with Bitter Greens and Sausage

The savouriness of pork sausage and the slight bitterness of rapini *make a great combination. If you cannot find* rapini, *try this recipe with any strong-tasting greens, such as cabbage greens together with dandelion leaves.*

INGREDIENTS

For 500g (1lb) *penne*

700g (1½lb) rapini **or** other bitter greens (see introductory note above)
250g (8oz) mild Italian pork sausage, crumbled, **or** homemade pork sausage (see recipe above)
90ml (6 tbsps) extra-virgin olive oil
1 tsp finely chopped garlic
salt and freshly ground black pepper
30g (1oz) butter
4 tbsps freshly grated pecorino romano cheese

PREPARATION

1 Trim the stems of the *rapini* or other greens and cook in salted boiling water until tender: about 5 minutes. Drain and, when cool enough to handle, coarsely chop.
2 Pour 4 litres (7 pints) of water into a large saucepan or pot and place over a high heat.
3 Put the sausage and about 60ml (4 tbsps) of water in a large sauté pan over a medium-high heat. As the sausage cooks, break it up with a wooden spoon. Once all the water has evaporated, let the sausage brown a little, then add another tablespoon of water and loosen any bits from the bottom of the pan with the spoon.
4 When the water for the pasta is boiling, add 1 tablespoon of salt and drop in the pasta all at once, stirring well.
5 Once all the water from the sauce has evaporated, add the olive oil and the garlic. Sauté until the garlic begins to change colour, then drop in the cooked greens and cook for 2–3 minutes. Season with salt and black pepper (bearing in mind that there will be salt and pepper in the sausage), remove from the heat and set aside.
6 When the pasta is cooked *al dente*, drain and toss with the sauce, adding the butter and the grated cheese. Serve at once.

Also good with: *conchiglie, lumache, fusilli corti*

MACCHERONI ALLA SALSICCIA E RICOTTA

Maccheroni with Sausage, Tomatoes and Ricotta

INGREDIENTS

For 500g (1lb) *maccheroni*

30g (1oz) butter
100g (3½oz) finely chopped onion
250g (8oz) mild Italian pork sausage, crumbled,
or *homemade pork sausage (see opposite)*
250g (8oz) tinned whole peeled tomatoes,
with their juice, coarsely chopped
salt and freshly ground black pepper
100g (3½oz) full-cream ricotta
2 tbsps freshly torn basil leaves
4 tbsps freshly grated parmigiano-reggiano *cheese*

PREPARATION

1 Melt the butter in a large sauté pan over a medium-high heat. Add the onion and cook until it softens and turns a rich golden colour.
2 Add the sausage and break it up with a wooden spoon. Cook until the sausage has browned lightly.
3 Stir in the tomatoes, season lightly with salt and black pepper (bearing in mind that there will be salt and pepper in the sausage) and continue cooking until the tomatoes have reduced and separated from the butter and sausage fat. Remove from the heat and set aside.
4 Meanwhile, bring 4 litres (7 pints) of water to the boil in a large saucepan or pot, add 1 tablespoon of salt and drop in the pasta all at once, stirring well.
5 When the pasta is almost done, return the pan with the sauce to a medium heat and add the *ricotta* and basil, mixing them in evenly.
6 When the pasta is cooked *al dente*, drain and toss with the sauce, adding the grated cheese. Serve at once.

Also good with: *penne, fusilli lunghi, fusilli corti, rigatoni, millerighe, elicoidali*

PENNE AL PROSCIUTTO E POMODORI SECCHI

Penne with Prosciutto, Sun-Dried Tomatoes and Cream

Jim Foley, who has worked with me as sous-chef, created this simple, tasty dish.

INGREDIENTS

For 500g (1lb) *penne*

30g (1oz) butter
60g (2oz) finely chopped onion
60g (2oz) prosciutto, cut from a 3mm (⅛in) thick slice
into thin strips
2 tbsps coarsely chopped sun-dried tomatoes in oil
250ml (8fl oz) double cream
salt
4 tbsps freshly grated parmigiano-reggiano *cheese*

PREPARATION

1 Pour 4 litres (7 pints) of water into a large saucepan or pot and place over a high heat.
2 Melt the butter in a large sauté pan over a medium-high heat. Add the onion and cook until it softens and turns a rich golden colour, then stir in the *prosciutto* and cook until it begins to brown.
3 When the water for the pasta is boiling, add 1 tablespoon of salt and drop in the pasta all at once, stirring well.
4 Meanwhile, add the sun-dried tomatoes and cream to the sauté pan with the onion and *prosciutto*, season lightly with salt and continue cooking until the cream has reduced by half. Remove from the heat and set aside.
5 When the pasta is cooked *al dente*, drain and toss with the sauce, adding the grated cheese. Taste for salt and serve at once.

Also good with: *farfalle, bucatini, garganelli*

117

Farfalle al salmone
(page 121)

Fusilli corti alle zucchine
(page 120)

Maccheroni alla
salsiccia e ricotta
(page 117)

FORME SPECIALI
Special Shapes

FUSILLI CORTI ALLE ZUCCHINE

Fusilli with Courgettes

INGREDIENTS

For 500g (1lb) *fusilli*

90ml (6 tbsps) extra-virgin olive oil
125g (4oz) very thinly sliced onion
1 tsp finely chopped garlic
1 tbsp finely chopped flat-leaf parsley
500g (1lb) courgettes, trimmed and cut into sticks 4cm
(1½in) long and 6mm (¼in) wide
2 tbsps shredded fresh basil
1 tsp finely chopped fresh mint
salt and freshly ground black pepper
4 tbsps freshly grated pecorino romano *cheese*

PREPARATION

1 Put the olive oil and onion in a large sauté pan over a medium-low heat. Cook, stirring occasionally, until the onion has softened and turned a rich golden colour.
2 Pour 4 litres (7 pints) of water into a large saucepan or pot and place over a high heat.
3 Raise the heat under the sauté pan to medium-high and add the garlic. Cook, stirring frequently, for about 1 minute, then add the parsley and the courgettes and stir well. Cook, stirring occasionally, until the courgettes are tender and lightly browned: 5 – 10 minutes.
4 Stir in the basil and the mint and season with salt and black pepper. Remove the pan from the heat and set aside.
5 When the water for the pasta is boiling, add 1 tablespoon of salt and drop in the pasta all at once, stirring well.
6 When the pasta is cooked *al dente*, drain and toss it with the sauce, adding the grated cheese. Serve at once.

Also good with: *fusilli lunghi, eliche*

ORECCHIETTE AL CAVOLFIORE

Orecchiette with Cauliflower and Pancetta

INGREDIENTS

For 500g (1lb) *orecchiette*

500g (1lb) cauliflower, leaves and stem removed
60ml (4 tbsps) extra-virgin olive oil
1 tsp finely chopped garlic
90g (3oz) pancetta, cut from a 6mm (¼in) thick slice
into thin strips
salt and freshly ground black pepper
4 tbsps freshly grated pecorino romano *cheese*

PREPARATION

1 Cook the cauliflower in abundant unsalted boiling water for 6 – 8 minutes or until tender. When cool enough to handle, cut it into 1cm (½in) pieces.
2 Pour 4 litres (7 pints) of water into a large saucepan or pot and place over a high heat.
3 Put the olive oil and garlic in a large sauté pan over a medium-high heat. When the garlic begins to sizzle, add the *pancetta* and sauté until it is browned but not crisp.
4 Turn the heat down to medium and stir in the cauliflower. Season with salt and black pepper and cook, stirring occasionally, until the cauliflower is lightly browned: 8 – 10 minutes. Remove the pan from the heat and set aside.
5 When the water for the pasta is boiling, add 1 tablespoon of salt and drop in the pasta all at once, stirring well.
6 When the pasta is cooked *al dente*, drain and toss with the sauce, adding the grated cheese. Serve at once.

Also good with: *fusilli corti, strozzapreti*

FARFALLE AL SALMONE

Bow-tie Pasta with Fresh Salmon

Salmon is not commonly used in Italy but in the Pacific Northwest of the US fresh salmon is abundant and very good. To take advantage of this popular native fish I devised the following recipe, which has had great success whenever I've served it.

INGREDIENTS

For 500g (1lb) *farfalle*

60ml (4 tbsps) extra-virgin olive oil
1 tsp finely chopped garlic
¼ tsp crushed chillies
500g (1lb) tinned whole peeled tomatoes,
with their juice, coarsely chopped
salt
250g (8oz) fresh boned salmon, cut into 1cm (½in) dice
250ml (8fl oz) double cream
2 tbsps shredded fresh basil

PREPARATION

1 Put the olive oil, garlic and crushed chillies in a large sauté pan over a medium-high heat and cook until the garlic begins to change colour.
2 Pour in the tomatoes and season with salt. When the tomatoes begin to bubble, turn the heat down to medium-low and cook until the tomatoes have reduced and separated from the oil: about 20 minutes. Remove from the heat and set aside.

You can prepare the sauce ahead of time up to this point and refrigerate or even freeze it.

3 Bring 4 litres (7 pints) of water to the boil in a large saucepan or pot, add 1 tablespoon of salt and drop in the pasta all at once, stirring well.
4 Return the pan with the tomato sauce to a medium-high heat and add the salmon, cream and a pinch of salt. Cook over a medium-high heat until the cream has reduced by half. Stir in the basil and remove from the heat.
5 When the pasta is cooked *al dente*, drain and toss with the sauce. Taste for salt and spiciness and serve at once.

Also good with: *penne*

FARFALLE AL SALMONE AFFUMICATO

Bow-tie Pasta with Smoked Salmon and Roasted Red Peppers

You need a smoked fish that you can flake for this recipe. If you cannot get thick, flakeable fillets of smoked salmon, use smoked trout fillets instead.

INGREDIENTS

For 500g (1lb) *farfalle*

2 red peppers
2 cloves garlic, peeled
250g (8oz) flakeable smoked salmon **or** trout fillet
(see introductory note above)
250ml (8fl oz) double cream
salt and freshly ground black pepper
2 tbsps shredded fresh basil

PREPARATION

1 Roast the peppers under the grill or over an open flame until the skin is charred on all sides. Place them in a bowl and cover the bowl tightly with cling film. After about 20 minutes take the peppers out, cut them in half, remove the core and scrape away the blistered skin and the seeds. Place the peppers and the garlic in a food processor or blender and grind until creamy. Remove and set aside.
2 Bring 4 litres (7 pints) of water to the boil in a large saucepan or pot, add 1 tablespoon of salt and drop in the pasta all at once, stirring well.
3 Flake the smoked fish with a fork. Put the fish, the pepper purée and the cream in a large sauté pan over a medium-high heat. Season with salt (remembering that the fish is already salty) and black pepper and cook until the cream has reduced by half. Stir in the basil and remove from the heat.
4 When the pasta is cooked *al dente*, drain and toss with the sauce. Taste for salt and pepper and serve at once.

Also good with: *penne, fusilli corti, conchiglie*

FUSILLI CORTI ALLA CAMPAGNOLA

Fusilli with Aubergine, Courgettes and Peppers

INGREDIENTS

For 500g (1lb) *fusilli*

120ml (8 tbsps) extra-virgin olive oil
100g (3½oz) thinly sliced onion
1 tsp finely chopped garlic
125g (4oz) peeled and diced aubergine
125g (4oz) diced courgette
1 red pepper or ½ a red and ½ a yellow pepper, cored
and seeded, peeled and cut into 2.5cm (1in) squares
salt
pinch of crushed chillies
250g (8oz) fresh ripe plum tomatoes, peeled, seeded and
cut into 1cm (½in) dice, or 125g (4oz) tinned whole
peeled tomatoes, with their juice, coarsely chopped

PREPARATION

1 Put the olive oil and onion in a large sauté pan over a medium heat and cook until the onion has softened and turned a rich golden colour.

2 Stir in the garlic, cook for 1 minute, then add the aubergine (do not worry if the aubergine soaks up all the oil, it will release it once it is cooked). Cover the pan and cook for about 5 minutes.

3 Pour 4 litres (7 pints) of water into a large saucepan or pot and place over a high heat.

4 Uncover the sauté pan and add the courgette and peppers to the aubergine. Season with salt and add the crushed chillies. Cook, stirring frequently, until the vegetables start to become tender: about 5 minutes.

5 When the water for the pasta is boiling, add 1 tablespoon of salt and drop in the pasta all at once, stirring well.

6 Meanwhile, add the tomatoes to the sauce and continue cooking until they have reduced and separated from the oil: about 5 minutes. Remove from the heat and set aside.

7 When the pasta is cooked *al dente*, drain and toss thoroughly with the sauce. Taste for salt and serve at once.

Also good with: *penne rigate, rigatoni, elicoidali, millerighe, fusilli lunghi*

Courgette

Aubergine

Garlic

Onion

Extra-virgin olive oil

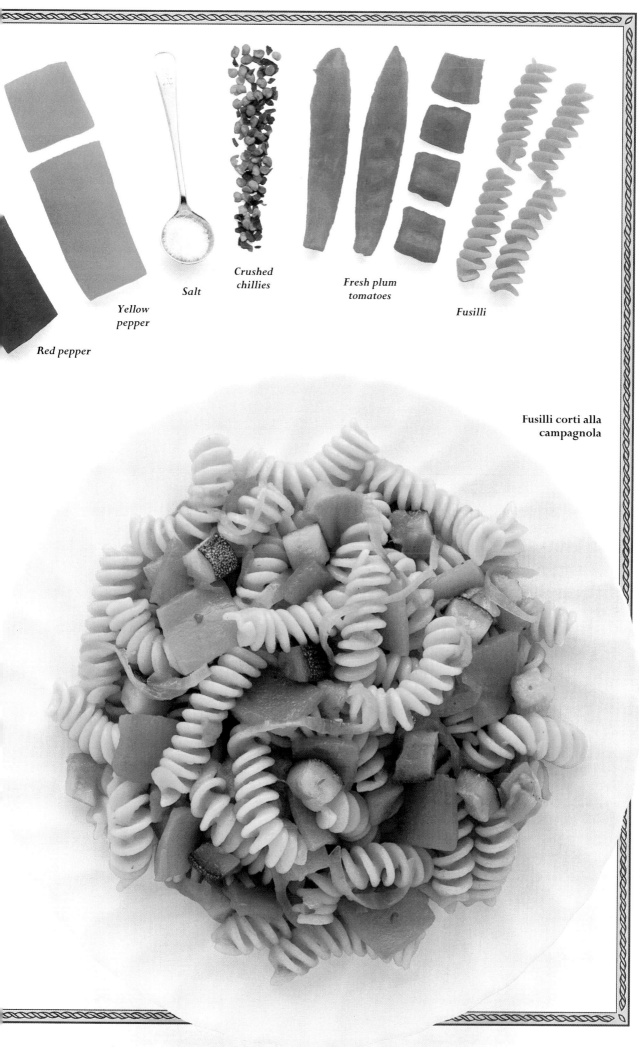

Red pepper

Yellow
pepper

Salt

Crushed
chillies

Fresh plum
tomatoes

Fusilli

**Fusilli corti alla
campagnola**

RUOTE DI CARRO CON PEPERONATA

Cartwheels with Peppers and Onions

INGREDIENTS

For 500g (1lb) *ruote di carro*

90ml (6 tbsps) extra-virgin olive oil
250g (8oz) thinly sliced onion
2 red and 2 yellow peppers, cored and seeded, peeled and cut lengthways into strips 6mm (¼in) wide
250g (8oz) tinned whole peeled tomatoes, with their juice, coarsely chopped
salt and freshly ground black pepper
pinch of crushed chillies
1 tbsp finely chopped flat-leaf parsley

PREPARATION

1 Put the olive oil and onion in a large sauté pan over a low heat. Cook, stirring occasionally, until the onion has wilted and turned golden in colour.

2 Turn the heat up to medium, add the peppers and cook, stirring frequently, until they soften slightly: about 2–3 minutes.

3 Pour in the tomatoes, season with salt and black pepper and add the crushed chillies. Stir well and cook until the tomatoes have reduced and separated from the oil: about 20 minutes.

4 Add the parsley, stir for about 30 seconds and remove from the heat. Set aside.

You can prepare the sauce ahead of time up to this point and refrigerate it.

5 Bring 4 litres (7 pints) of water to the boil in a large saucepan or pot, add 1 tablespoon of salt and drop in the pasta all at once, stirring well.

6 When the pasta is almost done, return the pan with the sauce to a medium heat.

7 Once the pasta is cooked *al dente*, drain and toss with the sauce. Taste for salt and serve at once.

Also good with: *rigatoni, penne rigate, fusilli lunghi, fusilli corti*

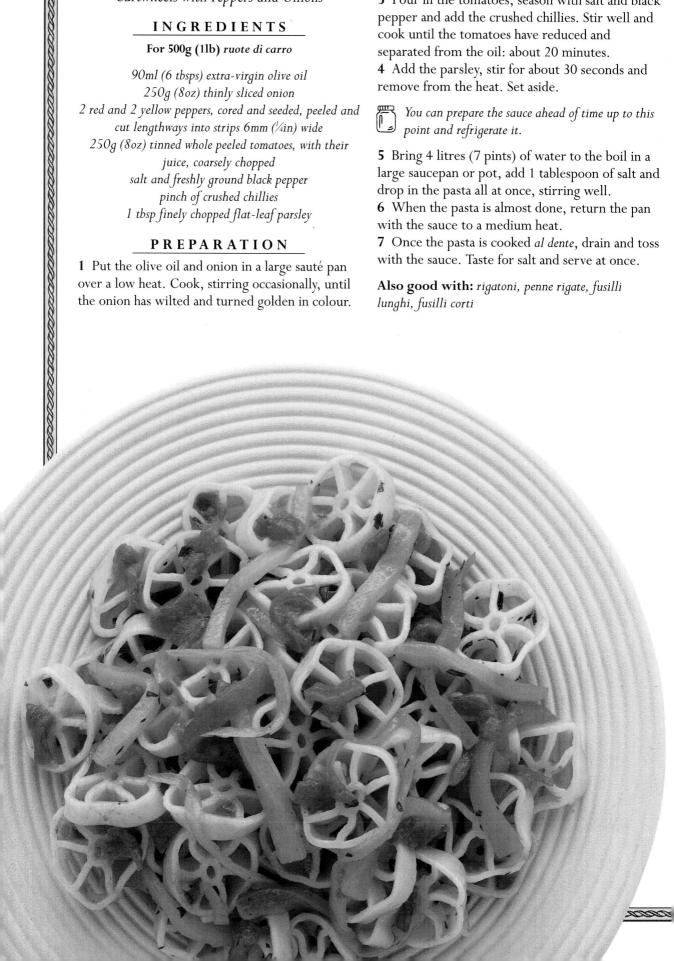

CONCHIGLIE ALLA SALSICCIA E PANNA

Shells with Sausages, Tomatoes and Cream

INGREDIENTS

For 500g (1lb) *conchiglie*

250g (8oz) mild Italian pork sausages
30g (1oz) butter
1 tsp fresh rosemary or ½ tsp dried, finely chopped
700g (1½lb) fresh ripe plum tomatoes, peeled,
seeded and cut into 1cm (½in) dice
pinch of crushed chillies
salt
120ml (8 tbsps) double cream
1 tbsp finely chopped flat-leaf parsley
4 tbsps freshly grated parmigiano-reggiano *cheese*

PREPARATION

1 Boil the sausages in water for 2–3 minutes. When they are cool enough to handle, slice them into thin rounds.

2 Pour 4 litres (7 pints) of water into a large saucepan or pot and place over a high heat.

3 Melt the butter in a large sauté pan over a medium-high heat. Add the sausage and cook until it is lightly browned.

4 Add the rosemary, tomatoes and 30ml (2 tbsps) of water. Cook until the water has evaporated and the tomatoes have just started to break down and form a sauce: about 5 minutes.

5 When the water for the pasta is boiling, add 1 tablespoon of salt and drop in the pasta all at once, stirring well.

6 Add the crushed chillies to the sauce in the sauté pan and season lightly with salt (bearing in mind that there will be salt in the sausage). Pour in the cream and sprinkle on the parsley. Cook, stirring frequently, until the cream has reduced by about half. Remove the pan from the heat and set aside.

7 When the pasta is cooked *al dente*, drain and toss with the sauce, adding the grated cheese. Taste for salt and spiciness and serve at once.

LUMACHE AI CARCIOFI

Lumache with Artichokes, Pancetta and Thyme

INGREDIENTS

For 500g (1lb) *lumache*

2 large artichokes
2 tbsps (30ml) lemon juice
60g (2oz) butter
100g (3½oz) finely chopped onion
125g (4oz) pancetta, *cut from a 1cm (½in) thick slice*
into thin strips
salt and freshly ground black pepper
½ tsp chopped fresh thyme or ¼ tsp dried
6 tbsps freshly grated parmigiano-reggiano *cheese*

PREPARATION

1 Trim the artichokes as shown, slice them thinly and place in a bowl with cold water and the lemon juice to prevent them from becoming brown.

2 Melt the butter in a large sauté pan over a medium heat. Add the onion and cook until it softens and turns a rich golden colour. Add the *pancetta* and continue sautéing until the *pancetta* is nicely browned but not crisp.

3 Pour 4 litres (7 pints) of water into a large saucepan or pot and place over a high heat.

4 Drain the artichoke slices, rinse them under cold water and add to the sauté pan. Season with salt and black pepper and sprinkle with thyme, then stir a couple of times to coat them. Pour in enough water to come 1cm (½in) up the side of the pan and cook uncovered until the artichokes are very tender: 10–15 minutes. You may need to add more water periodically. When done, remove from the heat and set aside.

5 When the water for the pasta is boiling, add 1 tablespoon of salt and drop in the pasta all at once, stirring well.

6 Once the pasta is almost done, return the sauce to the heat and boil away any excess liquid, leaving just a little moisture.

7 When the pasta is cooked *al dente*, drain and toss with the sauce, adding the grated cheese. Taste for salt and pepper and serve at once.

Also good with: *gnocchi, fusilli corti, fusilli lunghi, cavatappi, radiatori*

TRIMMING ARTICHOKES

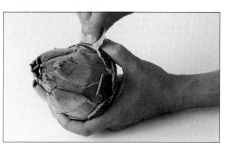

1 Remove the leaves of each artichoke by bending them back until they snap and pulling them down. The fresher the artichokes, the more easily the leaves will snap.

2 *Use a sharp knife to slice off the top. Discard it.*

3 *Scrape away the fuzzy choke from within the vegetable using a round knife such as a table knife.*

4 *Using a sharp paring knife, trim away all the dark green parts. Finally, cut off the stem, and the artichoke is ready for use.*

Lumache ai carciofi

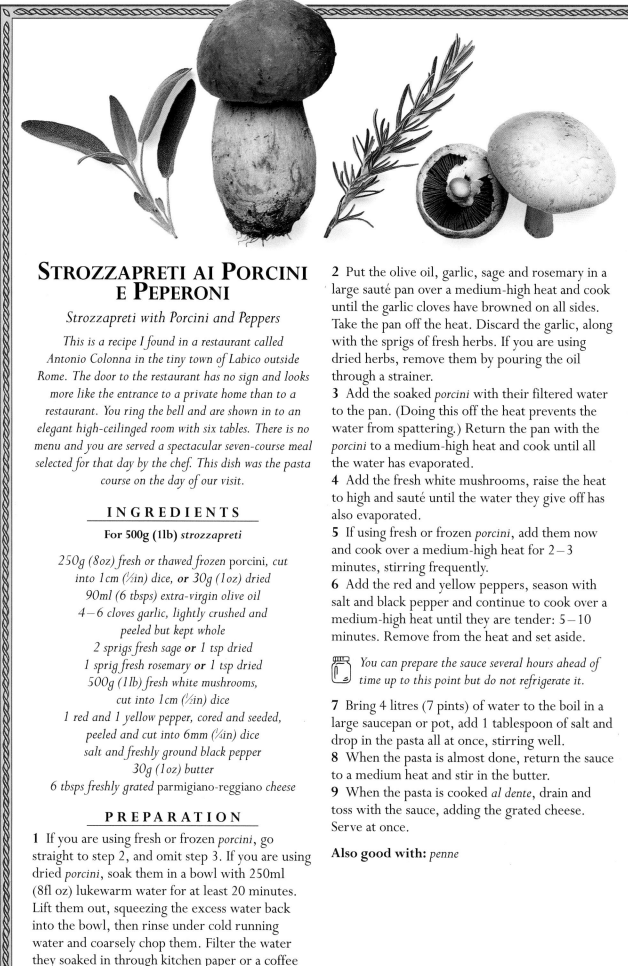

STROZZAPRETI AI PORCINI E PEPERONI

Strozzapreti with Porcini and Peppers

This is a recipe I found in a restaurant called Antonio Colonna in the tiny town of Labico outside Rome. The door to the restaurant has no sign and looks more like the entrance to a private home than to a restaurant. You ring the bell and are shown in to an elegant high-ceilinged room with six tables. There is no menu and you are served a spectacular seven-course meal selected for that day by the chef. This dish was the pasta course on the day of our visit.

INGREDIENTS

For 500g (1lb) *strozzapreti*

250g (8oz) fresh or thawed frozen porcini, *cut into 1cm (½in) dice,* **or** *30g (1oz) dried*
90ml (6 tbsps) extra-virgin olive oil
4–6 cloves garlic, lightly crushed and peeled but kept whole
2 sprigs fresh sage **or** *1 tsp dried*
1 sprig fresh rosemary **or** *1 tsp dried*
500g (1lb) fresh white mushrooms, cut into 1cm (½in) dice
1 red and 1 yellow pepper, cored and seeded, peeled and cut into 6mm (¼in) dice
salt and freshly ground black pepper
30g (1oz) butter
6 tbsps freshly grated parmigiano-reggiano *cheese*

PREPARATION

1 If you are using fresh or frozen *porcini*, go straight to step 2, and omit step 3. If you are using dried *porcini*, soak them in a bowl with 250ml (8fl oz) lukewarm water for at least 20 minutes. Lift them out, squeezing the excess water back into the bowl, then rinse under cold running water and coarsely chop them. Filter the water they soaked in through kitchen paper or a coffee filter and set aside.

2 Put the olive oil, garlic, sage and rosemary in a large sauté pan over a medium-high heat and cook until the garlic cloves have browned on all sides. Take the pan off the heat. Discard the garlic, along with the sprigs of fresh herbs. If you are using dried herbs, remove them by pouring the oil through a strainer.

3 Add the soaked *porcini* with their filtered water to the pan. (Doing this off the heat prevents the water from spattering.) Return the pan with the *porcini* to a medium-high heat and cook until all the water has evaporated.

4 Add the fresh white mushrooms, raise the heat to high and sauté until the water they give off has also evaporated.

5 If using fresh or frozen *porcini*, add them now and cook over a medium-high heat for 2–3 minutes, stirring frequently.

6 Add the red and yellow peppers, season with salt and black pepper and continue to cook over a medium-high heat until they are tender: 5–10 minutes. Remove from the heat and set aside.

You can prepare the sauce several hours ahead of time up to this point but do not refrigerate it.

7 Bring 4 litres (7 pints) of water to the boil in a large saucepan or pot, add 1 tablespoon of salt and drop in the pasta all at once, stirring well.

8 When the pasta is almost done, return the sauce to a medium heat and stir in the butter.

9 When the pasta is cooked *al dente*, drain and toss with the sauce, adding the grated cheese. Serve at once.

Also good with: *penne*

INSALATA DI FUSILLI E PENNE

Polly's Pasta Salad

When my wife, Polly, had to make a dish for a special party she had been invited to, she created this delicious pasta salad.

INGREDIENTS

For 250g (8oz) *fusilli corti* **and 250g (8oz)** *penne*

2 red peppers
1 medium-sized aubergine
90ml (6 tbsps) extra-virgin olive oil
90g (3oz) artichoke hearts, preserved in oil, quartered
8 – 10 green olives, flesh sliced from around stone
8 – 10 black olives, flesh sliced from around stone
2 tbsps capers
1 avocado, peeled and cut into 1cm (½in) chunks
15ml (1 tbsp) red wine vinegar
salt

PREPARATION

1 Roast the peppers under the grill or over an open flame until the skin is charred on all sides. Place in a bowl and cover the bowl tightly with cling film. After about 20 minutes take the peppers out, cut them in half, remove the core and scrape away the blistered skin and the seeds. Cut the flesh into 1cm (½in) squares.
2 Roast the aubergine whole in the same way as the peppers, but instead of covering it in a bowl leave it out on a plate. When it is cool enough to handle, cut off the top and peel away the skin. Cut it in half lengthways, remove most of the seeds and cut the flesh into 2cm (¾in) chunks.
3 Bring 4 litres (7 pints) of water to the boil in a large saucepan or pot, add 1 tablespoon of salt and drop in both pastas, stirring well (if they are the same brand, they will take the same amount of time to cook).
4 When the pasta is *molto al dente* (about 30 seconds away from being *al dente*), drain and toss in a bowl with 30ml (2 tbsps) of the olive oil.
5 Add the peppers, aubergine and the rest of the ingredients to the bowl, with the remainder of the olive oil and a sprinkling of salt. Toss well and set aside to cool completely before serving, but do not refrigerate.

ORECCHIETTE ALLA VERZA

Orecchiette with Anchovies and Savoy Cabbage

This recipe is also very good with broccoli: use 350g (12oz) chopped broccoli florets in place of 1kg (2lb) shredded cabbage. Don't cover the pan in step 3; turn the heat up to high instead, sauté the broccoli for 5 minutes only, and omit step 5.

INGREDIENTS

For 500g (1lb) *orecchiette*

120ml (8 tbsps) extra-virgin olive oil
4 cloves garlic, lightly crushed and peeled but kept whole
6 – 8 anchovy fillets, chopped
1kg (2lb) savoy cabbage, shredded
salt and freshly ground black pepper
30g (1oz) butter
6 tbsps freshly grated parmigiano-reggiano cheese

PREPARATION

1 Put the olive oil and garlic in a large sauté pan over a medium-high heat and cook until the garlic cloves have browned on all sides.
2 Discard the garlic. Turn the heat down to low and, once the oil has cooled slightly, add the anchovies (otherwise you may fry them). Cook, stirring with a wooden spoon, until the anchovies have dissolved.
3 Stir in the savoy cabbage, season with salt and black pepper and toss until the cabbage is well coated with the anchovy oil. Cover the pan and cook, stirring occasionally, until the cabbage is very tender: 20 – 30 minutes.
4 Pour 4 litres (7 pints) of water into a large saucepan or pot and place over a high heat.
5 Uncover the sauté pan and raise the heat to medium-high to evaporate any water from the sauce. Once the water has evaporated and the cabbage has coloured lightly, remove the pan from the heat and set aside.
6 When the water for the pasta is boiling, add 1 tablespoon of salt and drop in the pasta all at once, stirring well.
7 Once the pasta is almost done, return the sauce to a medium heat and stir in the butter.
8 When the pasta is cooked *al dente*, drain and toss with the sauce, adding the grated cheese. Serve at once.

Also good with: *fusilli corti, cavatappi, strozzapreti*

MINESTRE

Soup

BRODO DI CARNE

Homemade Meat Broth

A homemade Italian meat broth is delicate and light, made with a combination of raw meats and vegetables. Do not confuse it with stock, which is usually more intense and concentrated, made with oven-baked bones and vegetables.

INGREDIENTS

*2.5kg (5lb) beef and veal meat and bones
(you can also use chicken)
1 tsp salt
2 carrots, peeled
2 – 3 celery sticks
1 medium-sized onion, peeled
1 fresh ripe plum tomato or 1 whole tinned tomato
1 sprig flat-leaf parsley
1 tbsp whole black peppercorns*

PREPARATION

1 Put all the ingredients in a large stockpot, pour in enough cold water to cover by 5cm (2in) and place over a high heat.
2 When the water begins to boil, turn the heat down to very low and skim off the froth that has come to the surface. Place the cover on loosely so that it leaves a gap. Cook at a very gentle simmer for about 3 hours.
3 When the broth is done, pour it through a strainer and let it cool completely. It will keep in the refrigerator for 3 days. If you want to keep it for longer, it is best to freeze it. Pour the stock into ice-cube trays and, once it is frozen, store the cubes in plastic bags in the freezer.

MINESTRA DI PASTA E CECI

Pasta and Chickpea Soup

My mother's chickpea soup is perfect for a cold winter's evening and if you have tinned chickpeas you can produce it in less than 45 minutes from start to finish. The addition of homemade maltagliati *makes it even more delectable.*

INGREDIENTS

*90ml (6 tbsps) extra-virgin olive oil
4 cloves garlic, lightly crushed and peeled but kept whole
2 tsps fresh rosemary or 1 tsp dried, finely chopped
175g (6oz) tinned whole peeled tomatoes, with
their juice, coarsely chopped
350g (12oz) drained tinned chickpeas
700ml (1¼ pints) homemade meat broth (see left) or
1 beef bouillon cube dissolved in 700ml (1¼ pints) water
salt and freshly ground black pepper
250g (8oz) homemade* maltagliati *or any
small, tubular pasta
4 tbsps freshly grated* parmigiano-reggiano *cheese*

PREPARATION

1 Put the olive oil and garlic in a large, heavy-bottomed stockpot over a medium-high heat and cook until the garlic has browned on all sides.
2 Discard the garlic, then stir the rosemary into the oil. Remove the pot briefly from the heat and pour the tomatoes in. Reduce the heat to medium-low, return the pot and cook until the tomatoes have reduced and separated from the oil: 15 – 20 minutes.
3 Add the chickpeas, season with salt and black pepper, and cook for another 2 – 3 minutes.
4 Pour in the broth, cover the pot, and cook for 15 minutes more.
5 Use a slotted spoon to scoop up about a quarter of the chickpeas and either purée them through a food mill or mash them with a fork. Return them to the soup and raise the heat to medium-high. When the soup begins to boil, drop in the pasta and cover the pot.
6 When the pasta is *al dente*, take the soup off the heat and stir in the grated cheese. Let the soup rest for a few minutes before serving.

PASTA E FAGIOLI

Pasta and Bean Soup

There are many variations on the classic pasta and bean soup in Italy and my favourite is the one made in the Emilia-Romagna region. The best bean to use is the cranberry bean which is sometimes available fresh in the spring and summer though it is hard to find. Dried cranberry beans also work quite well provided they are soaked in water overnight, or you can use tinned cranberry beans or red kidney beans. This recipe is the classic method of preparing this soup, and I learned it from my mother.

INGREDIENTS

60ml (4 tbsps) extra-virgin olive oil, plus extra for serving with the soup
2 tbsps finely chopped onion
3 tbsps finely diced carrot
3 tbsps finely diced celery
3–4 pork ribs or 2 small pork chops
175g (6oz) tinned whole peeled tomatoes, with their juice, coarsely chopped
700ml (1¼ pints) fresh cranberry beans or tinned, drained cranberry or red kidney beans, or 350g (12oz) dried cranberry beans soaked overnight
1 litre (1¾ pints) homemade meat broth (see opposite) or 1 beef bouillon cube dissolved in 1 litre (1¾ pints) water
salt
250g (8oz) homemade maltagliati or any small, tubular pasta
4 tbsps freshly grated parmigiano-reggiano cheese
freshly ground black pepper

PREPARATION

1 Put the olive oil and onion in a large, heavy-bottomed stockpot over a medium heat and sauté until the onion turns a rich golden colour.
2 Stir in the carrot and celery and sauté for another 2 minutes. Add the pork and cook, stirring occasionally, for about 10 minutes.
3 Pour in the tomatoes, turn the heat down to low and simmer for about 10 minutes or, if you are using tinned beans in the next step, until the tomatoes have reduced: about 25 minutes.
4 Add the beans, stir well and add the broth. Cover the pot and cook until the beans are tender: about 45 minutes for fresh or dried-and-soaked beans, 5 minutes for tinned beans (which are already cooked).
5 Remove the pork (but don't discard it – it makes a great snack for the cook at this point!). Use a slotted spoon to scoop up about a quarter of the beans. Purée them through a food mill or mash them with a fork and return them to the pot. Season with salt (it's important not to add salt until the beans are fully cooked or the skins will become tough).

The soup may be prepared ahead of time up to this point and refrigerated.

6 Check the density of the soup. It should not be watery but have enough liquid for the pasta to cook in it. If necessary add a little more broth or water. Raise the heat to medium-high. When the soup begins to boil, drop in the pasta.
7 When the pasta is *al dente*, remove the soup from the heat and stir in the grated cheese. The soup is best if you allow it to rest for a few minutes before serving. Once it is ready to serve, ladle it into bowls and season each serving with black pepper and a light drizzle of fresh olive oil.

MINESTRINA DEI BAMBINI

Children's Soup with Pastina

In Italy this is traditionally a soup made for small children or for people who are convalescing and do not feel up to a regular meal. It is a comforting and revitalizing soup.

INGREDIENTS

1.25 litres (2¼ pints) homemade meat broth (see opposite) or 2 beef or chicken bouillon cubes dissolved in 1.25 litres (2¼ pints) water
175g (6oz) pastina (small pasta for soup)
30g (1oz) butter
4 tbsps freshly grated parmigiano-reggiano cheese

PREPARATION

1 Bring the broth to the boil. Drop in the *pastina* and cook briefly until *al dente*. Remove the pan from the heat.
2 Stir in the butter and the grated cheese and serve at once.

MINESTRA DI PASTA E VERDURE ALLA ROMANA

Roman Soup with Pasta and Vegetables

In an old Italian book on pasta I came across mention of a Roman soup made with pasta and "various lettuces". It sounded interesting so I decided to try making it with Swiss chard, kale, round lettuce and savoy cabbage. The result was a wonderful, elegant soup, which far exceeded my expectations.
Any tasty dark leafy cabbage works well here. Wash all leaves and remove any thick stalks before cooking. The total weight of leaves will be about 250g (8oz).

INGREDIENTS

30g (1oz) butter
45ml (3 tbsps) extra-virgin olive oil
60g (2oz) finely chopped onion
2 tbsps finely diced pancetta
4 tbsps finely diced carrot
4 tbsps finely diced celery
½ tsp fresh rosemary or ¼ tsp dried, finely chopped
2 handfuls of roughly chopped Swiss chard or (if chard is unavailable) spinach leaves
handful of roughly chopped kale or cabbage green leaves
2 handfuls of roughly chopped lettuce leaves
3 handfuls of finely shredded savoy cabbage leaves
salt and freshly ground black pepper
1.25 litres (2¼ pints) homemade meat broth
(see page 130) or 1 beef bouillon cube dissolved in
1.25 litres (2¼ pints) water
175g (6oz) tubetti, ditali or, my favourite, cavatappi
4 tbsps freshly grated parmigiano-reggiano cheese

PREPARATION

1 Put the butter, one third of the olive oil and all the onion in a large, heavy-bottomed stockpot over a medium-low heat.
2 When the onion has softened and turned a rich golden colour, stir in the *pancetta* and continue cooking until it is lightly browned but not crisp.
3 Add the carrot, celery and rosemary and sauté until they are lightly browned.
4 Drop in all the leaves and season with salt and black pepper. Once the leaves have wilted, continue sautéing for a further 2 minutes, then pour in the broth. When the broth begins to boil, turn the heat down to low and cover the pot. Cook for 1 hour.
5 Raise the heat to medium-high. When the soup begins to boil again, drop in the pasta and cover the pot. When the pasta is *al dente*, pour the soup into bowls. Drizzle the remaining olive oil over each serving and sprinkle each with the grated cheese. Serve at once.

Spinach

Fresh rosemary

Celery

Carrot

Pancetta

Onion

Extra-virgin olive oil

Butter

Kale

Lettuce

Savoy
cabbage

Salt

Black
pepper

Broth

Tubetti

Parmigiano-
reggiano

Minestra
alla romana

PASTA RIPIENA E AL FORNO
Stuffed and Baked Pasta

TORTELLONI DI BIETE

Tortelloni Filled with Swiss Chard

It is with these tortelloni *that my life-long love of pasta began. I prefer them with the simple butter and tomato sauce on page 52 but they are also wonderful with just butter and* parmigiano-reggiano *cheese. They are shown* di spinaci *(stuffed with spinach) on page 53.*

INGREDIENTS

THE TORTELLONI

1kg (2lb) Swiss chard (more if the stalks are large) **or**
fresh spinach **or** *625g (1¼lb) frozen spinach, thawed*
salt
60g (2oz) butter
4 tbsps finely chopped onion
60g (2oz) finely chopped prosciutto
200g (7oz) full-cream ricotta
1 egg yolk
60g (2oz) freshly grated parmigiano-reggiano *cheese*
⅛ tsp freshly grated nutmeg
pasta dough made with 2 eggs (see page 36)

THE SAUCE

Burro e pomodoro *sauce (see page 52), made in advance,* **or** *90g (3oz) butter, cut into small pieces*
60g (2oz) freshly grated parmigiano-reggiano *cheese*

PREPARATION

THE TORTELLONI

1 If using fresh chard or spinach leaves, remove the stalks or stems and wash the leaves in several changes of cold water. Place them in a pan over a medium-high heat with ½ teaspoon of salt and just the water that clings to them after washing. Cover and cook until the leaves are tender: about 8 – 12 minutes. If using frozen spinach, cook it for about 3 minutes in salted boiling water to cover.
2 Drain the leaves and, when cool enough to handle, squeeze out excess water and chop.
3 Melt the butter in a sauté pan over a medium heat. Add the onion and cook until it turns a rich golden colour. Add the *prosciutto* and sauté for 1 minute. Add the Swiss chard or spinach and cook, stirring, for 3 minutes (do not worry if it absorbs all the butter). Transfer to a bowl. Allow to cool.
4 Mix in the *ricotta*, egg yolk, grated cheese and nutmeg. Combine thoroughly, and taste for salt.

5 Roll out the pasta dough as thinly as possible and make the stuffed *tortelloni* as shown on page 42. Spread them out on a clean tea towel.
6 Bring 4 litres (7 pints) of water to the boil in a large saucepan or pot, add 1 tablespoon each of salt and of olive oil, and slide in the pasta using the tea towel it was spread out on.
7 Gently reheat the *Burro e pomodoro* sauce, or melt the butter.
8 When the sealed edges of the *tortelloni* are cooked *al dente*, drain them and transfer to a serving dish. Pour the sauce or melted butter over them, sprinkle on the grated cheese and gently toss until the pasta is evenly coated. Serve at once.

TORTELLINI ALLA PANNA

Tortellini with Cream

There is a story that tells of a pasta-maker secretly in love with a young girl who worked for him. Before she started work she would change her clothes in the back room, and one day the owner gave in to the temptation to peek through the keyhole. All he could see was her navel but he found it so beautiful that he picked up a small disk of pasta and mimicked its shape. This, so legend has it, is how the first tortellino *was born.*

INGREDIENTS

THE TORTELLINI

15g (½oz) butter
15ml (1 tbsp) vegetable oil
60g (2oz) lean boneless pork loin,
cut into 1cm (½in) cubes
salt and freshly ground black pepper
90g (3oz) boneless, skinless chicken breast, trimmed of all fat, and cut into 1cm (½in) cubes
60g (2oz) very finely chopped mortadella
150g (5oz) full-cream ricotta
1 egg yolk
¼ tsp freshly grated nutmeg
60g (2oz) freshly grated parmigiano-reggiano *cheese*
pasta dough made with 2 eggs (see page 36)

THE SAUCE

30g (1oz) butter
120ml (8 tbsps) double cream
6 tbsps freshly grated parmigiano-reggiano *cheese*

PREPARATION

THE TORTELLINI

1 Put the butter, oil and pork in a sauté pan over a medium heat. Season with salt and black pepper and cook, stirring, for 5 minutes. Remove the pork with a slotted spoon and set aside.

2 Add the chicken to the sauté pan, season with salt and black pepper, and cook, stirring, for 2 – 3 minutes. Remove with a slotted spoon and set aside together with the pork.

3 Chop the pork and chicken finely (but not to a paste) in a food processor or by hand. Transfer to a bowl and, using a fork, mix in the *mortadella*, *ricotta*, egg yolk, nutmeg and grated cheese. Knead to amalgamate the ingredients thoroughly. Taste for salt and set aside.

4 Roll out the pasta dough as thinly as possible and make the stuffed *tortellini* as shown on page 42. Spread them out on a clean tea towel.

THE SAUCE

1 Pour 4 litres (7 pints) of water into a large saucepan or pot and place over a high heat.

2 Melt the butter for the sauce in a large sauté pan over a medium-high heat. Pour in the cream and cook, stirring frequently, until the cream has reduced by half. Remove the pan from the heat and set aside.

3 When the water for the pasta is boiling, add 1 tablespoon each of salt and of olive oil, and slide in the pasta using the tea towel it was spread out on.

4 When the sealed edges of the *tortellini* are cooked *al dente*, return the pan with the sauce to a low heat, drain the *tortellini* and toss very gently with the cream and butter sauce in the pan, adding the grated cheese, a pinch of salt and some grindings of black pepper. Taste for seasoning and serve at once.

**Tortellini
alla panna**

TORTELLONI DI RICOTTA E PREZZEMOLO

Tortelloni Filled with Ricotta and Parsley

*These tortelloni are a speciality of Bologna. Unlike the
pillow-shaped versions elsewhere in this section,
Bolognese tortelloni are shaped like large cappelletti.
The best sauce is the pink tomato sauce used in the recipe
for Tortelloni di carciofi (page 138).*

INGREDIENTS

300g (10oz) full-cream ricotta
60g (2oz) finely chopped flat-leaf parsley
1 egg yolk
⅛ tsp freshly grated nutmeg
125g (4oz) freshly grated parmigiano-reggiano cheese
salt and freshly ground black pepper
pasta dough made with 2 eggs (see page 36)

PREPARATION

1 In a mixing bowl, use a fork to combine the
ricotta, parsley, egg yolk, nutmeg and half of the
grated cheese. Season with salt and black pepper.
2 Roll out the pasta dough as thinly as possible and
make the stuffed *tortelloni* as shown on page 43.
Spread them out on a clean tea towel.
3 Prepare the pink tomato sauce as in the recipe
for *Tortelloni di carciofi* on page 138.
4 Bring 4 litres (7 pints) of water to the boil in a
large saucepan or pot, add 1 tablespoon each of
salt and of olive oil, and slide in the pasta using the
tea towel it was spread out on.
5 When the sealed edges of the *tortelloni* are
cooked *al dente*, drain and transfer to a serving
dish. Pour the sauce over them and gently toss
with the remaining grated cheese. Serve at once.

RAVIOLINI DI PESCE AL SUGO DI GAMBERI

Seafood Raviolini with Prawn Sauce

INGREDIENTS

THE RAVIOLINI

30g (1oz) butter
½ tsp fresh marjoram *or* ¼ tsp dried, finely chopped
250g (8oz) bass *or* similar delicate white fish, boned
and skinned
salt and freshly ground black pepper
125g (4oz) loose scallops, without coral
30ml (2 tbsps) double cream
2 egg yolks
3 tbsps freshly grated parmigiano-reggiano cheese
pinch of freshly grated nutmeg
pasta dough made with 2 eggs (see page 36)

THE SAUCE

90ml (6 tbsps) extra-virgin olive oil
3 cloves garlic, lightly crushed and peeled but kept whole
2 tbsps tomato purée
120ml (8 tbsps) dry white wine
250g (8oz) medium-sized prawns, peeled and
deveined if necessary
salt and freshly ground black pepper
250ml (8fl oz) double cream
2 tbsps finely chopped flat-leaf parsley

PREPARATION

THE RAVIOLINI

1 Put the butter in a sauté pan over a medium-
high heat and allow it to foam. When the foam
begins to subside, add the marjoram and the fish.
Cook the fish on both sides, taking care not to
overcook it or it will become dry: 4–6 minutes.
Season with salt and black pepper and remove
from the pan using a slotted spoon.
2 Put the cooked fish in a food processor or
blender, chop until almost creamy, then transfer
to a mixing bowl.
3 Put the raw scallops in the processor or blender
and chop them very finely. Add the cream and run
the machine for about 5 more seconds. Transfer to
the mixing bowl with the fish.
4 Add the egg yolks, grated cheese and nutmeg to
the mixture in the bowl. Combine thoroughly
with a fork and taste for salt and black pepper.
5 Roll out the pasta dough as thinly as possible
and make the stuffed *raviolini* as shown on page 43.
Spread them out on a clean tea towel.

**Raviolini di pesce
al sugo di gamberi**

THE SAUCE

1 Put the olive oil and garlic in a sauté pan over a medium-high heat. When the garlic cloves have browned on all sides, remove and discard them. Remove the pan from the heat.

2 Dissolve the tomato purée in the white wine and pour into the pan. Return to a medium-high heat and reduce the wine by three-quarters.

3 Add two-thirds of the prawns to the pan. Cook, stirring, until they have turned pink: about 2 – 3 minutes. Season with salt and black pepper.

4 Turn off the heat under the pan and remove the prawns using a slotted spoon. Put them in a food processor, chop them very finely and return them to the pan. Turn the heat to medium-high again and add half the cream. Cook, stirring often, until it has reduced by half. Remove from the heat.

5 Pour 4 litres (7 pints) of water into a large saucepan or pot and place over a high heat.

6 Cut the remaining raw prawns into thirds. Return the sauce to a medium-high heat and add the remaining cream and the cut raw prawns. Cook, stirring frequently, until the newly added cream has reduced by half, then stir in the parsley. If the sauce appears to curdle at any point, it will correct itself if stirred well. Remove from the heat and set aside.

7 When the water for the pasta is boiling, add 1 tablespoon each of salt and of olive oil, and slide in the pasta from the tea towel.

8 When the sealed edges of the *raviolini* are cooked *al dente*, drain and transfer to a serving dish. Pour the sauce over them and gently toss until the pasta is evenly coated. Serve at once.

TORTELLONI DI CARCIOFI ALLA PANNA ROSA

Artichoke Tortelloni with Pink Tomato Sauce

INGREDIENTS

THE TORTELLONI

2 large or 3 medium-sized artichokes
30ml (2 tbsps) lemon juice
45g (1½oz) butter
3 tbsps finely chopped onion
salt and freshly ground black pepper
1 egg yolk
60g (2oz) freshly grated parmigiano-reggiano cheese
⅛ tsp freshly grated nutmeg
pasta dough made with 2 eggs (see page 36)

THE SAUCE

½ quantity of Burro e pomodoro sauce (see page 52), made in advance
120ml (8 tbsps) double cream
60g (2oz) freshly grated parmigiano-reggiano cheese

PREPARATION

THE TORTELLONI

1 Trim the artichokes as shown on pages 126–7, slice thinly and place in a bowl of cold water with the lemon juice to prevent them from browning.
2 Melt the butter in a large sauté pan over a medium heat. Add the onion and cook until it softens and turns a rich golden colour.
3 Drain the artichokes, rinse and add to the pan. Stir to coat well, season with salt and black pepper and pour in water to come 1cm (½in) up the side of the pan. Cook, uncovered, until the water has evaporated and the artichokes are very tender, adding more water if needed: 10–15 minutes.
4 Transfer to a food processor or blender and chop until creamy. Allow to cool in a mixing bowl.
5 Add the egg yolk, grated cheese and nutmeg to the bowl. Mix thoroughly with a fork.
6 Roll out the pasta dough as thinly as possible and make the *tortelloni* as shown on page 42. Spread on a clean tea towel.

THE SAUCE

1 Pour 4 litres (7 pints) of water into a large saucepan or pot and place over a high heat.
2 Pass the *Burro e pomodoro* sauce through a food mill or a sieve then heat in a sauté pan over a medium-low heat until it begins to bubble.
3 Add the cream, raise the heat to medium and cook until the sauce is thick enough to coat a metal spoon: 2–3 minutes. Take off the heat.
4 When the water for the pasta is boiling, add 1 tablespoon each of salt and of olive oil, and slide in the pasta from the tea towel.

5 When the sealed edges of the *tortelloni* are cooked *al dente*, drain them and transfer to a serving dish. Pour the sauce over them, sprinkle on the grated cheese and gently toss until the pasta is evenly coated. Serve at once.

TORTELLI ALLA FERRARESE

Pasta Squares Filled with Sweet Potato

Tortelli filled with sweet local pumpkin is a speciality of Ferrara in Emilia-Romagna. Outside Italy, orange-fleshed sweet potato is generally the best substitute for Italian pumpkin. The sauce I like best for these is butter and sage, but plain butter works well too.

INGREDIENTS

THE TORTELLI

250g (8oz) orange-fleshed sweet potatoes
vegetable oil for brushing
3 tbsps finely chopped prosciutto
1 egg yolk
125g (4oz) freshly grated parmigiano-reggiano cheese
3 tbsps finely chopped flat-leaf parsley
⅛ tsp freshly grated nutmeg
salt and freshly ground black pepper
pasta dough made with 2 eggs (see page 36)

THE SAUCE

2 tbsps finely shredded fresh sage leaves (optional)
90g (3oz) butter, cut into small pieces
60g (2oz) freshly grated parmigiano-reggiano cheese

PREPARATION

THE TORTELLI

1 Preheat the oven to 200°C/400°F/gas 6.
2 Brush the sweet potatoes with vegetable oil and place them on a baking sheet in the oven. Cook until they are very tender and the skin feels as if it has separated from the flesh (cooking time will vary depending on the size of the potatoes). Remove from the oven and peel as soon as they are cool enough to handle.
3 Work them through a food mill or purée in a food processor. Allow to cool in a mixing bowl.
4 Add the *prosciutto*, egg yolk, grated cheese, parsley and nutmeg, season with salt and black pepper, and mix thoroughly with a fork.

You can prepare the filling 1 day ahead and refrigerate it.

5 Roll out the pasta dough as thinly as possible and make the stuffed *tortelli* following the instructions given for *tortelloni* on page 42. Spread them out on a clean tea towel.

THE SAUCE

1 Pour 4 litres (7 pints) of water into a large saucepan or pot and place over a high heat.

2 Melt the butter in a small saucepan over a medium heat. Season lightly with salt and black pepper. Either remove from the heat and set aside, or, if you are using sage, stir in the sage now, cook for 1–2 minutes until the butter just begins to darken, then set aside.

3 When the water for the pasta is boiling, add 1 tablespoon each of salt and of olive oil, and slide in the pasta from the tea towel.

4 When the sealed edges of the *tortelli* are cooked *al dente*, drain and transfer to a serving dish. Pour the sauce over them and gently toss until the pasta is coated, adding the grated cheese. Serve at once.

ROTOLO DI PASTA

Baked Sliced Pasta Roll Filled with Spinach

This elegant and delicious pasta dish comes from the Emilia-Romagna region of Italy and is a recipe I learned from my mother. It is perfect for a dinner party because you can prepare it ahead of time up to the point when it goes in the oven.

INGREDIENTS

THE ROTOLO

1kg (2lb) fresh spinach or 600g (1¼lb) frozen spinach, thawed
salt
60g (2oz) butter
4 tbsps finely chopped onion
60g (2oz) finely chopped prosciutto
200g (7oz) full-cream ricotta
150g (5oz) freshly grated parmigiano-reggiano *cheese*
pinch of freshly grated nutmeg
1 egg yolk
pasta dough made with 2 eggs (see page 36)

THE SAUCE

½ quantity of béchamel sauce (see page 142)
½ quantity of Burro e pomodoro *sauce (see page 52), made in advance*

PREPARATION

THE ROTOLO

1 If using fresh spinach, remove the stalks and wash the leaves in several changes of cold water. Place them in a pan over a medium-high heat with ½ teaspoon of salt and just the water that clings to them after washing. Cover and cook until the leaves are tender: 8–12 minutes. If using frozen spinach, cook for about 3 minutes in salted boiling water to cover. Drain and, when cool enough to handle, squeeze out the water and coarsely chop.

2 Melt the butter in a sauté pan over a medium heat. Add the onion and cook until it softens and turns a rich golden colour. Stir in the *prosciutto* and sauté for 1 more minute. Add the spinach and sauté for another 3 minutes (do not worry if the spinach absorbs all the butter). Transfer to a mixing bowl and allow to cool.

3 Add the *ricotta*, all but 4 tablespoons of the grated cheese, the nutmeg and the egg yolk to the bowl. Mix with a fork, then knead with your hands to amalgamate the ingredients. Taste for salt and set aside.

4 Roll out the pasta dough, either by hand or through the pasta machine. Trim hand-rolled pasta into a rectangle of about 30 x 40cm (12 x 16in). If using machine-rolled pasta, lay three strips, approximately 40cm (16in) long, side by side and slightly overlapping. Moisten the overlapping edges with water and seal them together.

5 Using a rubber spatula, spread the spinach filling over the pasta, no more than 3mm (⅛in) deep. Leave 1cm (½in) clear along the edges. Roll the pasta sheet and filling like a Swiss roll, pinch the ends shut, then wrap it tightly in muslin or cheesecloth, tying the ends with string.

6 Bring 4 litres (7 pints) of water to the boil in a large saucepan or pot, add 1 tablespoon of salt and gently immerse the pasta roll. Cook it at a steady boil for 20 minutes then lift it out carefully using two tongs or large spoons, unwrap it, and allow it to cool.

TO ASSEMBLE AND BAKE

1 Make the béchamel sauce according to the recipe on page 142. Mix it with the *Burro e pomodoro* sauce.

2 Preheat the oven to 200°C/400°F/gas 6, unless assembling the dish in advance to cook later.

3 Cut the cooled pasta roll with a sharp knife into 1cm (½in) slices.

4 Spread a little of the béchamel and tomato mixture on the bottom of a shallow baking dish. Lay the pasta-roll slices on top, overlapping them like tiles if necessary.

5 Cover the pasta-roll slices with the rest of the béchamel and tomato mixture. Top with the remaining grated cheese.

You may assemble the dish ahead of time up to this point and bake it later.

6 Place on the upper shelf of the preheated oven. Bake for about 15–20 minutes or until a light crust forms on top. Remove from the oven and allow to rest for 10 minutes before serving.

Lasagne coi gamberi
e canestrelli
(page 142)

Rotolo di pasta
(page 139)

Tortelli alla ferrarese
with butter and sage sauce
(page 138)

Lasagne coi Gamberi e Canestrelli

Lasagne with Prawns and Scallops

INGREDIENTS

45ml (3 tbsps) extra-virgin olive oil
4 tbsps finely chopped onion
1 tsp finely chopped garlic
1 tbsp finely chopped flat-leaf parsley
250g (8oz) loose scallops, cut into 6mm (¼in) pieces
250g (8oz) medium-sized raw prawns, peeled, deveined
if necessary and cut into 6mm (¼in) pieces
salt and freshly ground black pepper
1 quantity of béchamel sauce (see right)
pasta dough made with 2 eggs (see page 36)

PREPARATION

1 Put the olive oil and onion in a sauté pan over a medium heat and cook until the onion softens and turns a rich golden colour. Add the garlic and parsley and cook for about another minute.

2 Turn the heat up to medium-high and add the scallops. When they are no longer translucent and any water they release has evaporated (about 1 minute), add the prawns, season with salt and black pepper and cook until the prawns turn pink. Remove from the heat.

TO ASSEMBLE AND BAKE

1 Make the béchamel sauce according to the recipe (see right).

2 Pour 4 litres (7 pints) of water into a large saucepan or pot and place over a high heat. Place a large bowl filled with cold water, ice and a sprinkling of salt near the cooker and spread out some clean, dry tea towels.

3 Roll out the pasta dough as thinly as possible. Cut it into strips 10cm (4in) wide and shorter than the shallow baking dish you plan to use.

4 When the water is boiling, add 1 tablespoon of salt. Drop 4 pasta sheets at a time into the boiling water. Cook very briefly (about 1 minute), taking them out with a slotted spoon while still very *al dente* and placing them in the iced water. Swish about to remove excess starch, then lay the sheets in a single layer on the tea towels. Pat them dry. Continue until you have cooked all the pasta.

5 Preheat the oven to 200°C/400°F/gas 6.

6 Smear the bottom of the baking dish with some of the béchamel sauce and mix the remainder with the seafood sauce. Line the bottom of the dish with a layer of pasta strips and spread just enough of the béchamel and seafood mixture over the pasta layer to cover it.

7 Continue layering the pasta and the sauce until there are at least 5 layers. Spread sauce thinly over the top layer of pasta.

8 Place on the upper shelf of the oven. Bake for about 15–20 minutes or until a light golden crust forms on top. Remove from the oven and allow to rest for 10 minutes before serving.

Balsamella

Béchamel Sauce

INGREDIENTS

500ml (⅘ pint) full-cream milk
60g (2oz) butter
4 level tbsps plain flour
salt and freshly ground black or white pepper

PREPARATION

1 Heat the milk until it begins to bubble. Remove from the heat.

2 Meanwhile, melt the butter in a heavy-bottomed saucepan over a medium-low heat. Sprinkle on the flour, mixing with a wire whisk until it is smooth. Let it cook for 1–2 minutes, stirring constantly, and taking care not to let it brown.

3 Begin adding the hot milk, a few tablespoons at a time, whisking the mixture smooth before adding more. When the consistency becomes quite thin you can start adding milk more rapidly. Continue until all the milk has been mixed in.

4 Continue cooking over a medium-low heat, stirring constantly with the whisk, until the sauce begins to thicken. The sauce is done when it coats the whisk thickly. Season with salt and black or white pepper before removing from the heat. Béchamel sauce is best when used the same day but it keeps overnight in the refrigerator if necessary.

LASAGNE ALLE ZUCCHINE

Lasagne with Courgettes

INGREDIENTS

1.3kg (3lb) courgettes (if yellow courgettes are available, use half green and half yellow)
30ml (2 tbsps) extra-virgin olive oil
30g (1oz) butter
1 tsp finely chopped garlic
1 tbsp finely chopped flat-leaf parsley
½ tsp fresh thyme or ¼ tsp dried, finely chopped
salt and freshly ground black pepper
1½ quantities of béchamel sauce (see opposite)
⅛ tsp freshly grated nutmeg
90g (3oz) freshly grated parmigiano-reggiano cheese
pasta dough made with 2 eggs (see page 36)

PREPARATION

1 Trim the courgettes and cut them in half lengthways. Lay the halves cut-side down, and slice crossways into 6mm (¼in) semi-circles.
2 Put the olive oil, butter and garlic in a large sauté pan over a medium-high heat. When the garlic begins to change colour, add the parsley and thyme and stir well.
3 Mix in the courgettes, season with salt and black pepper and continue cooking, stirring from time to time, until tender and lightly browned. Remove the courgette and herb mixture using a slotted spoon and set it aside.
4 Make the béchamel sauce according to the recipe (see opposite). Pour about four-fifths of it into a bowl, add the courgette and herb mixture, the nutmeg and 60g (2oz) of the grated cheese, and stir.

TO ASSEMBLE AND BAKE

1 Roll out, cut and part-cook the pasta dough, following the instructions for *Lasagne coi gamberi e canestrelli*, opposite (steps 2 to 4).
2 Preheat the oven to 200°C/400°F/gas 6.
3 Smear the bottom of the baking dish with half the remaining béchamel sauce and cover with a layer of pasta. Cover the pasta with a thin layer of the béchamel and courgette sauce.
4 Continue layering the pasta and the sauce until there are at least 5 layers. Spread the remaining béchamel and the remaining sauce over the top layer of pasta so that it is dotted with courgette. Sprinkle the remaining grated cheese on top.
5 Place on the upper shelf of the oven. Bake for about 15 – 20 minutes or until a light golden crust forms on top. Remove from the oven and allow to rest for 10 minutes before serving.

LASAGNE ALLA BOLOGNESE

Lasagne with Meat Bolognese Sauce

INGREDIENTS

1 quantity of Ragù sauce, made in advance (see page 62)
1½ quantities of béchamel sauce (see opposite)
pasta dough made with 2 eggs (see page 36)
salt
90g (3oz) freshly grated parmigiano-reggiano cheese
30g (1oz) butter

PREPARATION

1 Place the *ragù* in a mixing bowl.
2 Make the béchamel sauce according to the recipe (see opposite).

TO ASSEMBLE AND BAKE

1 Roll out, cut and part-cook the pasta dough, following the instructions for *Lasagne coi gamberi e canestrelli*, opposite (steps 2 to 4).
2 Preheat the oven to 200°C/400°F/gas 6, unless assembling the dish in advance to cook later.
3 Smear the bottom of a baking dish with some of the béchamel sauce and cover with a layer of pasta strips. Mix the rest of the béchamel with the meat sauce and spread a thin layer over the pasta.
4 Continue layering the pasta and the béchamel and meat sauce until there are at least 5 layers. Spread the remaining sauce thinly over the top layer of pasta. Sprinkle the grated cheese on top and dot with the butter.

 You can assemble the dish ahead of time and refrigerate it for up to 2 days.

5 Place on the upper shelf of the oven. Bake for about 15 – 20 minutes or until a light golden crust forms on top. Remove from the oven and allow to rest for 10 minutes before serving.

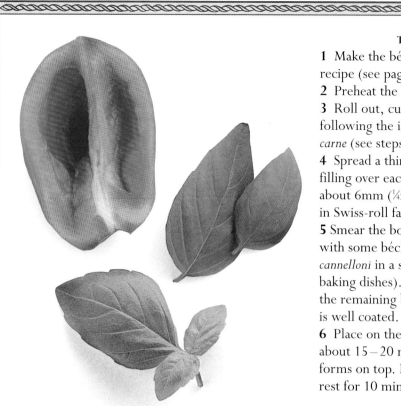

TO ASSEMBLE AND BAKE

1 Make the béchamel sauce according to the recipe (see page 142).
2 Preheat the oven to 200°C/400°F/gas 6.
3 Roll out, cut and part-cook the pasta dough, following the instructions given for *Cannelloni di carne* (see steps 3 to 5, opposite).
4 Spread a thin layer of the tomato and cheese filling over each rectangle, leaving a border of about 6mm (¼in) all round. Roll up the *cannelloni* in Swiss-roll fashion.
5 Smear the bottom of a suitably sized baking dish with some béchamel sauce and arrange the *cannelloni* in a single layer (if necessary use two baking dishes). Cover the top of the *cannelloni* with the remaining béchamel, making sure all the pasta is well coated. Sprinkle the grated cheese on top.
6 Place on the upper shelf of the oven. Bake for about 15–20 minutes or until a light golden crust forms on top. Remove from the oven and allow to rest for 10 minutes before serving.

CANNELLONI ALLA SORRENTINA

Cannelloni Filled with Fresh Tomatoes, Mozzarella and Basil

INGREDIENTS

30g (1oz) butter
2 tbsps finely chopped onion
700g (1½lb) fresh ripe plum tomatoes, peeled, seeded and cut into 6mm (¼in) dice
salt and freshly ground black pepper
2 tbsps shredded fresh basil
125g (4oz) fresh mozzarella
100g (3½oz) full-cream ricotta
½ quantity of béchamel sauce (see page 142)
pasta dough made with 2 eggs (see page 36)
4 tbsps freshly grated parmigiano-reggiano cheese

PREPARATION

1 Melt the butter in a sauté pan over a medium heat. Add the onion and cook until it softens and turns a rich golden colour.
2 Raise the heat to medium-high, add the tomatoes, season with salt and black pepper and cook until the tomatoes have reduced and separated from the butter: about 10–15 minutes.
3 Stir in the basil, cook for another 2 minutes then remove from the heat. Transfer the contents of the pan to a mixing bowl.
4 While the tomato and basil mixture is still warm, add the *mozzarella* and *ricotta*. Combine with a fork and taste for salt and pepper.

CANNELLONI DI CARNE

Meat-Filled Cannelloni

These are a speciality of Lombardy in northern Italy. Preparing them is time-consuming but really quite simple. Cannelloni should not be tubes, but rectangles of homemade pasta spread with filling and rolled up. This recipe is essentially the way my mother makes them.

INGREDIENTS

60g (2oz) butter
3 tbsps finely chopped onion
350g (12oz) lean minced beef
salt and freshly ground black pepper
250g (8oz) tinned whole peeled tomatoes, with their juice, coarsely chopped
100g (3½oz) very finely chopped mortadella
1 egg yolk
⅛ tsp freshly grated nutmeg
275g (9oz) full-cream ricotta
150g (5oz) freshly grated parmigiano-reggiano cheese
1 quantity of béchamel sauce (see page 142)
pasta dough made with 2 eggs (see page 36)

PREPARATION

1 Put 30g (1oz) butter in each of two saucepans and melt it over a medium heat. Divide the onion between them and sauté to a rich golden colour.
2 Divide the minced beef between the pans and cook, crumbling with a wooden spoon, until it has lost its raw colour. Add salt and black pepper.

3 Add the tomatoes to one of the pans and, as soon as they have started to bubble, reduce the heat to a mere simmer. Cook until the tomatoes have reduced and separated from the butter: about 35–45 minutes. (This is the meat sauce.)

4 Cook the meat in the other pan for just a few minutes after it has lost its raw colour, then take it off the heat. Remove the meat from the pan using a slotted spoon and place in a mixing bowl.

5 When the meat in the mixing bowl has cooled completely, add the *mortadella*, egg yolk, nutmeg, *ricotta* and 125g (4oz) of the grated cheese. Mix well with a fork. (This is the filling.)

You can prepare the filling and the meat sauce 1 day ahead and refrigerate them.

TO ASSEMBLE AND BAKE

1 Make the béchamel sauce according to the recipe (see page 142), reducing the cooking time to achieve a thinner sauce.

2 Preheat the oven to 200°C/400°F/gas 6.

3 Pour 4 litres (7 pints) of water into a large saucepan or pot and place over a high heat. Place a large bowl filled with cold water, ice and a sprinkling of salt near the cooker and spread out some clean, dry tea towels.

4 Roll out the pasta dough as thinly as possible and cut into rectangles of 7.5 x 10cm (3 x 5in).

5 When the water is boiling, add 1 tablespoon of salt and drop in as many rectangles of pasta as will comfortably float in the water. Cook very briefly (about 30 seconds), taking them out with a slotted spoon while still very *al dente* and placing them in the iced water. Once all the rectangles are cooked, swish them about in the iced water then remove them with a slotted spoon and place in a single layer on the tea towels. Pat them dry.

6 Add about 6 tablespoons of the béchamel to the filling, mixing it in well. Spread a thin layer of the filling over each rectangle, leaving a border of about 6mm (¼in) all round. Roll up the *cannelloni* in Swiss-roll fashion.

7 Smear the bottom of a suitably sized baking dish with some béchamel sauce and arrange the *cannelloni* in a single layer (if necessary use two baking dishes). Cover the top of the *cannelloni* with the meat sauce and the rest of the béchamel, making sure all the pasta is well coated. Sprinkle the remaining grated cheese on top.

8 Place on the upper shelf of the oven. Bake for about 15–20 minutes or until a light golden crust forms on top. Remove from the oven and allow to rest for 10 minutes before serving.

PIZZA DI MACCHERONI

Maccheroni "Pizza" with Tomatoes and Parmigiano-Reggiano Cheese

This unusual pasta dish is a speciality of the Principe restaurant in Pompei. It is meant to be eaten cold but I find it is also good warm.

INGREDIENTS

For 400g (14oz) *maccheroni*

60ml (4 tbsps) extra-virgin olive oil
½ tsp finely chopped garlic
700g (1½lb) fresh ripe plum tomatoes
cut into 6mm (¼in) dice
salt and freshly ground black pepper
60g (2oz) freshly grated parmigiano-reggiano *cheese*
2 eggs
30g (1oz) butter

PREPARATION

1 Pour 4 litres (7 pints) of water into a large saucepan or pot and place over a high heat.

2 Put the olive oil and garlic in a sauté pan over a medium-high heat and cook until the garlic begins to change colour.

3 Pour in the tomatoes and cook until they have reduced and separated from the oil: 10–15 minutes. Season with salt and black pepper, remove from the heat and transfer to a mixing bowl large enough to accommodate the pasta later.

4 When the water for the pasta is boiling, add 1 tablespoon of salt and drop in the pasta all at once, stirring well.

5 When the pasta is *molto al dente* (about 1 minute away from being *al dente*), drain and toss in the bowl with the sauce. Mix in the grated cheese and allow the pasta to cool down.

6 Beat the eggs and mix them in with the pasta.

7 Melt the butter in a large nonstick sauté pan over a medium heat and allow it to foam. When the butter foam begins to subside, pour in the pasta mixture, pressing it down with a spoon until it is quite compact. Cook until the bottom forms a golden-brown crust.

8 Remove from the heat, place a large flat plate upside down over the pan, then turn the pan over, allowing the "pizza" to loosen on to the plate. You can allow the "pizza" to cool completely before serving, or try it lukewarm.

Also good with: *penne, elicoidali*

RIGATONI AL FORNO AI PORCINI

Baked Rigatoni with Porcini Mushrooms

INGREDIENTS

For 400g (14oz) *rigatoni*

30g (1oz) dried porcini
60g (2oz) butter, plus extra for the baking dish
30ml (2 tbsps) vegetable oil
6 tbsps finely chopped onion
*125g (4oz) tinned whole peeled tomatoes, with their
juice, coarsely chopped*
500g (1lb) fresh white mushrooms, thinly sliced
2 tbsps finely chopped flat-leaf parsley
salt and freshly ground black pepper
⅔ quantity of béchamel sauce (see page 142)
6 tbsps freshly grated parmigiano-reggiano cheese

PREPARATION

1 Soak the dried *porcini* in a bowl with 250ml (8fl oz) lukewarm water for at least 20 minutes. Lift them out, squeezing the excess water back into the bowl, then rinse under cold running water and coarsely chop them. Filter the water they soaked in through kitchen paper or a coffee filter and set aside.
2 Put 45g (1½oz) of the butter and all the oil and onion in a large sauté pan over a medium heat and sauté until the onion has softened and turned a rich golden colour. Pour in the tomatoes and the reconstituted *porcini* with their filtered water. Cook, stirring occasionally, until the liquid in the pan has evaporated completely.
3 Raise the heat to medium-high, add the fresh mushrooms and parsley and season with salt and black pepper. Cook until all the water the mushrooms release has evaporated. Transfer to a bowl.
4 Make the béchamel sauce according to the instructions (see page 142). Add to the mushroom mixture in the bowl and mix in well.
5 Preheat the oven to 200°C/400°F/gas 6.
6 Bring 4 litres (7 pints) of water to the boil in a large saucepan or pot, add 1 tablespoon of salt and drop in the pasta all at once, stirring well.
7 When the pasta is *molto al dente* (about 1 minute away from being *al dente*), drain and toss with the sauce and 4 tablespoons of the grated cheese. Transfer to a greased baking dish and top with the remaining cheese and butter.
8 Place on the upper shelf of the oven. Bake for about 15–20 minutes or until a light golden crust forms on top. Remove from the oven and allow to rest for 10 minutes before serving.

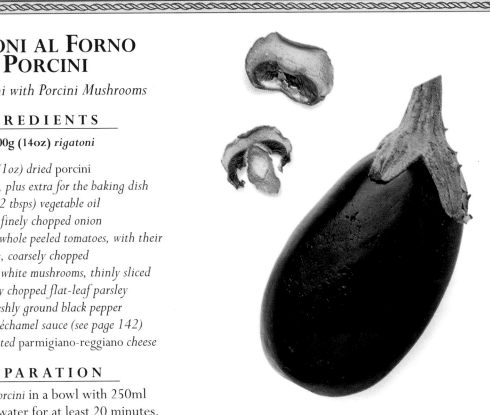

MACCHERONI AL FORNO ALLA RUSTICA

*Baked Maccheroni with Aubergine and
Smoked Mozzarella*

INGREDIENTS

For 400g (14oz) *maccheroni*

vegetable oil
1 aubergine, peeled and cut into 6mm (¼in) thick slices
salt
60g (2oz) butter, plus extra for the baking dish
125g (4oz) thinly sliced onion
*350g (12oz) tinned whole peeled tomatoes, with their
juice, coarsely chopped*
freshly ground black pepper
4 tbsps freshly grated parmigiano-reggiano cheese
*125g (4oz) Italian smoked mozzarella (use fresh if
smoked is unavailable), very thinly sliced*

PREPARATION

1 Pour vegetable oil into a sauté pan until it comes 1cm (½in) up the side. Place over a high heat. Once the oil has become very hot, carefully slip in as many slices of aubergine as will comfortably fit. As the bottom of each slice turns golden brown, turn it over, and when both sides are golden brown, remove from the pan and transfer to a plate covered with kitchen paper. Continue frying until all the aubergine is done. Sprinkle with salt.

2 Pour 4 litres (7 pints) of water into a large saucepan or pot and place over a high heat.

3 Melt the butter in another sauté pan over a medium heat. Add the onion and cook until it softens and turns a rich golden colour.

4 Add the tomatoes, season with salt and black pepper and cook until the tomatoes have reduced and separated from the butter. Remove from the heat and set aside.

5 Preheat the oven to 200°C/400°F/gas 6.

6 When the water for the pasta is boiling, add 1 tablespoon of salt and drop in the pasta all at once, stirring well.

7 When the pasta is *molto al dente* (about 1 minute away from being *al dente*), drain and toss with the sauce and the grated *parmigiano-reggiano* cheese.

8 Smear the bottom of a shallow baking dish with butter and pour in about half the pasta, spreading it out evenly. Cover with all the aubergine slices and half the *mozzarella* slices. Pour in the remaining pasta, and place the rest of the *mozzarella* slices on top.

9 Place on the upper shelf of the oven. Bake for about 15–20 minutes or until a light golden crust forms on top. Remove from the oven and allow to rest for 10 minutes before serving.

Maccheroni al forno alla rustica

TORTA RICCIOLINA

Angel Hair Pasta and Almond Pie

This is a recipe my mother learned from a friend of ours, Margherita Simili, who is a fabulous Bolognese baker. The pie is intended to resemble noodles with Bolognese meat sauce – the cocoa-covered almond mixture representing the meat. The dessert is not simply an interesting conversation piece but an excellent moist pie, definitely worth making. The original recipe calls for crystallized citron, which I have never been very fond of, so I've substituted homemade crystallized oranges, which I find more appealing.

INGREDIENTS

CRYSTALLIZED ORANGES
1 unpeeled orange, ends removed, cut in thin crosswise slices and seeds removed
75g (2½oz) granulated sugar, plus more as needed

PIE CRUST
175g (6oz) plain flour
6 level tbsps icing sugar
salt
2 egg yolks
90g (3oz) butter, cut into small pieces and softened to room temperature, plus extra for the cake tin

FILLING
200g (7oz) blanched almonds
150g (5oz) granulated sugar
1 tsp unsweetened, good quality cocoa
½ tsp grated lemon peel
pasta dough made with 2 eggs (see page 36)
125g (4oz) butter
60ml (4 tbsps) dark rum

PREPARATION

CRYSTALLIZED ORANGES
1 Put the orange slices, sugar and 60ml (4 tbsps) of water in a sauté pan large enough to fit them in with minimum overlapping. Cook over a medium-low heat for about 15–20 minutes until the orange pith becomes translucent and tender, adding more water if necessary.
2 When the oranges are done, continue cooking until all the water has evaporated and the sugar has formed a thick syrup, coating the orange slices and giving them a glossy look.
3 Sprinkle sugar on a plate large enough to fit all the orange slices without overlapping (use 2 plates if necessary). Lay the slices on the sugar and cover them with more sugar. Allow to cool completely.

You can prepare the oranges several days ahead of time and refrigerate them.

PIE CRUST
1 Mix the flour, icing sugar and a tiny pinch of salt on a pastry board or work surface. Make a well in the centre of the heaped flour mixture.
2 Put the egg yolks and butter in the well and work the flour into them, kneading into a smooth ball of dough. Wrap in cling film and refrigerate for 1 hour.

TO ASSEMBLE AND BAKE
1 Put the almonds, orange slices and granulated sugar in a food processor and chop to a medium-fine consistency. Transfer to a mixing bowl and add the cocoa and lemon peel, mixing well.
2 Preheat the oven to 190°C/375°F/gas 5.
3 Lightly grease a 20cm (8in) springform tin with butter, dust it with flour and tap it upside down to remove any excess flour.

4 Dust the pastry board or work surface with flour and roll out the pastry into a large circle approximately 6mm (¼in) thick. Using the rolling pin, lift the pastry on to the springform tin, letting it drape over the bottom and the sides to line the tin. Trim the edges level with the top of the tin. (If the pastry breaks up, you can patch it together and it will still taste good.)

5 Roll out the pasta dough as thinly as possible. When it is dry enough, roll it up and cut it into the narrowest possible noodles (following the instructions on page 40). Fluff up the noodles to prevent them from sticking together and proceed quickly to the next step before they have a chance to dry out completely.

6 Put one-third of the noodles into the tin, leaving them fluffed up. Set aside 6 tablespoons of the almond mixture and sprinkle half of the remainder over the pasta. Dot with a third of the butter. Put in another third of the pasta, sprinkle the other half of the almond mixture on top and dot with another third of the butter. Add the remaining pasta, sprinkle the reserved almond mixture over it and dot with the remaining butter.

7 Place the pie on the top shelf of the oven. After 15 minutes remove it from the oven and cover with baking parchment or aluminium foil. Return to the oven and bake for 25 more minutes.

8 Take the pie out of the oven, remove the paper or foil and immediately sprinkle with the rum. Let it cool completely before serving. It will keep refrigerated for up to 10 days.

PREPARING VEGETABLES

These are the basic techniques for peeling, cutting, dicing and chopping vegetables. When using a knife, choose one with a sharp blade. A dull blade requires the use of more force and is consequently harder to control. Keep your fingers bent away from the path of the knife.

PEELING A FRESH PEPPER

1 Slice the pepper in half along one of its ridges. With a circular movement, cut out the stalk and core. Tap each half cut-side down to dislodge the seeds.

2 Cut down the ridges of each pepper half. This enables you to cut away the pith and gives a smooth surface on which it easier to use the peeler.

3 Using a swivel-bladed peeler with a side-to-side, sawing motion, peel the top of each piece, then remove the rest of the skin by peeling downwards.

CUTTING A COURGETTE

1 Top and tail each courgette and slice in half lengthways. With the courgette cut-side down, and using the end of the blade, slice into long wedges.

2 Hold the wedges together and slice them crossways into pieces. Rest the knife blade against your knuckles and bend your fingers away from the knife.

DICING A CARROT

1 Lay a peeled carrot flat on the cutting board and cut horizontally into three or four slices, depending on the thickness of the carrot.

2 Stack two or more of the slices and cut them into long thin sticks, holding the carrot with your fingers bent away from the knife.

3 Line up the sticks and slice them crossways into small dice. Keep your fingers bent, with the flat of the blade against your knuckles.

PEELING A TOMATO

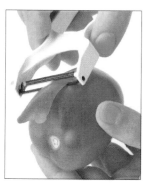

1 Peel the tomato using a swivel-bladed peeler. Use a side-to-side, sawing motion at the same time as you peel downwards.

2 Halve the tomato. Scoop out the seeds with your thumb and discard them. Coarsely chop the tomato flesh.

CHOPPING AN ONION

1 Top and tail the onion and slice in half from top to bottom. Remove the skin. With the cut side down, slice lengthways, leaving the root end intact.

2 Slice thinly crossways until you reach the end that is intact. Chop up the last piece, then chop all the onion together as finely as necessary.

TIPS

• You can dice a stick of celery in the same way as you would a carrot. First peel the outer part of the stick to remove the tough strings. Flatten the stick by pressing it down on the work surface with your hand.

• To dice a mushroom, remove the cap from the stem. Lay the cap flat on the cutting board and make two or three parallel cuts. Holding it together with your fingers, turn it a quarter turn and slice two or three more times. Cut the stem into pieces of the same size.

THE STORECUPBOARD

The ingredients here and overleaf are to be found in the well-stocked kitchen of any pasta-lover in Italy. If you build up a storecupboard of these items, you will never be stuck for a quick and satisfying meal, and could even put together a feast at short notice. Store items in their original packaging, and if necessary transfer from pantry to refrigerator once opened.

SHORT-NOTICE MEALS

Aglio e olio (page 48)

Burro e pomodoro (page 52)

Pomodoro e basilico (page 54)

Arrabbiata (page 56)

Puttanesca (page 58)

Puttanesca bianca (page 89)

IN THE PANTRY

These items either keep for a long time or else are so often used that if you cook Italian food on a regular basis they will never go to waste. Keep them in store along with a selection of your favourite dried pastas.

"OO" FLOUR
This flour is used in Bologna to make pasta. It is widely exported, and worth tracking down. If you cannot find "OO" flour, use unbleached plain flour instead. It also achieves good results.

PORCINI
Fresh porcini are increasingly hard to find but the dried versions are a readily available, flavourful alternative. They last forever, either in the original packaging or re-wrapped in cling film. Look for packets with large slices of whole mushrooms and beware of lower-priced ones that are mostly stems.

GARLIC
Buy fresh, firm heads of garlic and store in a cool, dry place. They should stay fresh for about two weeks.

Capers packed in vinegar

Salted capers

CAPERS
Available in salt or wine vinegar: salted ones have the purest flavour. Refrigerate them after opening.

ANCHOVIES
Look for flat fillets of anchovies in olive oil, in a tin or a jar, and refrigerate them after opening.

NUTMEG
Buy nutmeg whole and grate it finely the moment you need it. Its flavour is powerful so use it sparingly.

JUNIPER BERRIES
Dry juniper berries (probably best known for making gin) have a unique flavour that is wonderfully suited to robust meats, such as lamb.

CRUSHED CHILLIES
These are used not only for hot and spicy dishes but also sometimes, in very small amounts, to liven up a dish without making it hot.

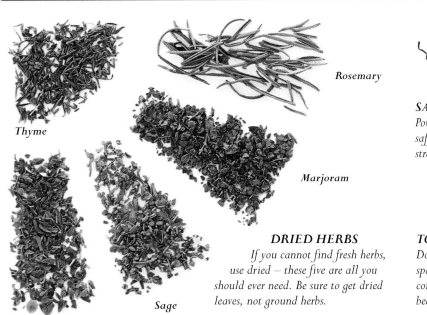

Thyme

Rosemary

Marjoram

Sage

Oregano

SAFFRON

Powder imparts the most flavour but saffron is most commonly available in strands. Finely chop strands before use.

DRIED HERBS

If you cannot find fresh herbs, use dried — these five are all you should ever need. Be sure to get dried leaves, not ground herbs.

TOMATO PUREE

Double concentrate is best, but use it sparingly. Tubes are the most convenient packaging for tomato purée because they can be easily resealed.

TINNED TOMATOES

The best are Italian plum tomatoes from San Marzano. Always use whole peeled tomatoes. They should have a fairly firm texture and a sweet ripe flavour without being too salty.

SUN-DRIED TOMATOES

These are available either dried or partly reconstituted in oil. If you buy the dried ones, soak them in water overnight, then squeeze out the excess water and store them in olive oil.

BALSAMIC VINEGAR

True balsamic vinegar is at least 50 years old and exorbitant in price. For ordinary use buy commercial balsamic vinegar and look for one that is richly flavoured, not too acid nor too sweet.

OLIVES

Outside Italy, good black olives to use are Greek ones. For green olives look for the large meaty southern Italian ones. Avoid pitted olives in tins because they are usually quite bland.

OLIVE OIL

There are several grades of olive oil: extra-virgin is the highest grade and pure is the lowest. Extra-virgin oil is obtained from the first press of the olives and without the use of heat. I recommend using extra-virgin olive oil and no other. The quality of all the ingredients you use is important in Italian cooking but olive oil is probably the one that makes the most difference to how well a dish turns out.

BASICS

Salt

Pepper

Onions

Dried breadcrumbs

White wine

IN THE REFRIGERATOR

You don't need a great deal of space or money to have the basics to hand for a wide variety of pasta sauces. Buy the cheeses and the meat from a good Italian food shop to be sure of having the real thing. Buy fresh herbs from a shop that has a quick turnover.

BASIL
Store this in the same way as parsley. Wait until you are ready to use it before you tear or cut it because it quickly wilts and blackens.

PARSLEY
Flat-leaf parsley keeps in a jar of water in the refrigerator. Detach the leaves from the stem, wash and spin them dry before chopping.

PARMIGIANO-REGGIANO
True parmigiano-reggiano is a cheese of incomparable quality, flavour and texture, which has been made in the same way for over 700 years. If you buy it in a big chunk, cut it into smaller pieces, wrap each tightly with cling film and then with foil, store in the refrigerator and it will keep for several months. Use one piece at a time and grate it only just before serving.

PECORINO ROMANO
This is a hard, sheep's milk cheese, aged for about one year and used for grating. It is sharper than parmigiano-reggiano, so use it in smaller quantities. Stored like parmigiano it will also keep for a long time.

RICOTTA
This is a cheese made from whey (the residue from the making of other cheeses) and it is creamy in texture and delicate in flavour. The best and creamiest is imported from Italy. If you cannot find imported ricotta, mix a small amount of cream into the locally made version.

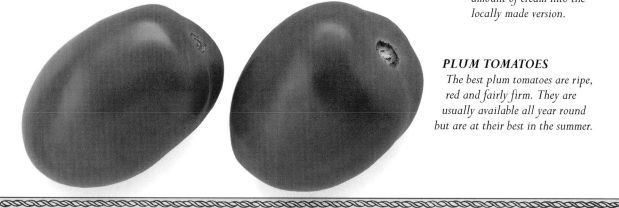

PLUM TOMATOES
The best plum tomatoes are ripe, red and fairly firm. They are usually available all year round but are at their best in the summer.

Slab pancetta

PANCETTA
This is the same cut of pork as bacon and it is cured like prosciutto *(see below) but aged for less time. It is leaner than bacon and usually unsmoked.*

Rolled pancetta

PROSCIUTTO
This is an air- and salt-cured ham which is aged for one year. If Italian prosciutto *is not available or is too expensive, look for a locally made version that is rich in flavour and not too salty.*

SAUCES YOU CAN REFRIGERATE

Arrabbiata
(page 56)

Amatriciana
(page 84)

Boscaiola
(page 110)

Pollo
(page 112)

Salmone
(page 121)

Peperonata
(page 124)

IN THE FREEZER

Frozen spinach is useful to keep in store. It is quicker and easier to use than fresh for homemade green pasta and, with *ricotta*, for stuffings, though fresh leaves are better for sauces.

When basil is plentiful, make a large batch of *pesto* and freeze it. The fresh leaves themselves cannot be frozen and thawed successfully. You can also make your own Italian-style sausage meat and freeze it; see *Salsiccia di maiale* on page 116.

Ragù and *Burro e pomodoro* sauces freeze well. It is a good idea to make more than you need and freeze the rest as a standby. So too with *Brodo* (page 130): you are bound to make more than you need at any one time so freeze the extra.

SAUCES YOU CAN FREEZE

Pesto di basilico
(page 50)

Burro e pomodoro
(page 52)

Ragù
(page 62)

Pomodoro
(page 88)

NOTES

AL DENTE, MOLTO AL DENTE

These terms, important in pasta cookery, translate literally as: "to the tooth" and "very much to the tooth". No Italian will cook pasta until it is soft and soggy: it is ready when it is still slightly firm and offers some resistance to the bite when you eat it. The stage of *molto al dente* comes around 30 to 90 seconds before *al dente* (depending on the pasta). Recipes ask for pasta to be *molto al dente* when it is not to be eaten immediately and will finish cooking either in the oven or in the pan.

OILS

Occasionally a recipe calls for vegetable oil instead of olive oil. Olive oil is used wherever it contributes to the flavour of the dish, but where its only function would be to prevent butter from burning during frying, vegetable oil is adequate. There is no point in wasting good-quality extra-virgin olive oil.

PARMESAN
PARMIGIANO-REGGIANO

Parmesan is a general name for a type of Italian cheese of which the original and best is *parmigiano-reggiano*. The production of true *parmigiano-reggiano* is limited by law to a relatively small area in the region of Emilia-Romagna, whose environment accounts for the particular flavour of its milk. The method of production is also regulated by law and each wheel of cheese, which must be aged a minimum of 18 months before being sold, is inspected before it receives the stamp of approval on its side. The best way to buy the cheese is in chunks taken straight from the wheel, whose stamp of approval is visible. Avoid Parmesan in packets, especially ready grated. It bears no resemblance to the real thing.

SALT

Although I have not indicated amounts for salt in the recipes, it should not be considered an optional ingredient (except, of course, for sound medical reasons). Salt is essential in bringing out the flavour of food and a properly salted dish will be rich in flavour without tasting salty. You can test this by taking two glasses of wine and putting a little salt into one. Smell the wine and you will notice how much fuller and more intense is the smell of the one with salt.

SAUCEPAN SIZE

You need a generously sized saucepan or pot for cooking pasta. It should accommodate all the water required for the quantity of pasta (see page 45) and still have room for the water to bubble up and the pasta to move around. Stir occasionally while cooking to prevent the pasta from sticking. You don't need to add olive oil except when cooking stuffed pasta.

SPOON SIZE

The recipes in this book use a standard tablespoon: 15ml (½fl oz). Avoid big, old-fashioned tablespoons, which measure 20ml or more. A standard teaspoon is 5ml.

TIMING

If in any doubt over how long a sauce will take to cook, finish it before you start the pasta. Pasta does not take long to cook, and should never be overcooked, while a sauce can be reheated, or cooked slowly at the end. Pasta must be tossed with sauce the moment it is drained.

WEIGHTS AND MEASURES

Both metric and imperial measures are given. To prevent confusion, follow either one set or the other. All the measures are rounded up and down to make them convenient and easy to use. Tablespoon measures are given for small quantities of dry ingredients, such as chopped onions, for greater accuracy.

OVEN TEMPERATURES		
110°C	225°F	gas ¼
120°C	250°F	gas ½
140°C	275°F	gas 1
150°C	300°F	gas 2
160°C	325°F	gas 3
180°C	350°F	gas 4
190°C	375°F	gas 5
200°C	400°F	gas 6
220°C	425°F	gas 7
230°C	450°F	gas 8
250°C	475°F	gas 9
260°C	500°F	gas 10

INDEX

ACKNOWLEDGMENTS

Author's appreciation

First and foremost, my parents, Victor and Marcella Hazan. I could not have written this book without their inspiration, support and all that they have taught me through the years.

My wife, Polly, for her love, her excellent palate which was invaluable when I was testing recipes, and her proofing and coaching of my prose.

Jenifer Lang, for recommending me to DK for this project.

Robert Lescher, for his encouragement and confidence in me.

Mari Roberts, Tracey Clarke, Carolyn Ryden and all the staff at DK in London for their excellent work in putting together this book and their patience with me; Lyn Rutherford for producing the dishes for photography; Clive Streeter and Amanda Heywood for their beautiful photographs; Pamela Thomas and Jeanette Mall and the staff at DK in New York for all their help and support.

Christy McCartney and Leroy Kunert for testing my recipes; the staff at Perlina Restaurant in Portland, Oregon for giving me ideas for some of the recipes in this book; Alberto Consiglio's book, *I Maccheroni*, which describes the legend of Chico, the Neapolitan magician.

And last, but not least, all the chefs and cooks I have had the fortune of meeting in my travels in Italy.

Dorling Kindersley would like to thank Lyn Rutherford for preparing the food that appears throughout the book; Meg Jansz for preparing food on pages 135, 140–1, 147, 148–9; Steve Gorton for additional photography (pages 2, 3, 4, 5, 6); Steven Begleiter for the photographs on pages 7 and 8; Sarah Ponder for the artworks; Alexa Stace for editorial assistance; Hilary Guy for help in styling pages 32–3 and 70–1; Deborah Rhodes for help with page make-up; Sarah Ereira for the index; Carluccio's of Neal Street, London and Mauro's of Muswell Hill Broadway, London for fresh pasta for catalogue photography; and Patricia Roberts and Frederick Hervey-Bathurst for additional props.

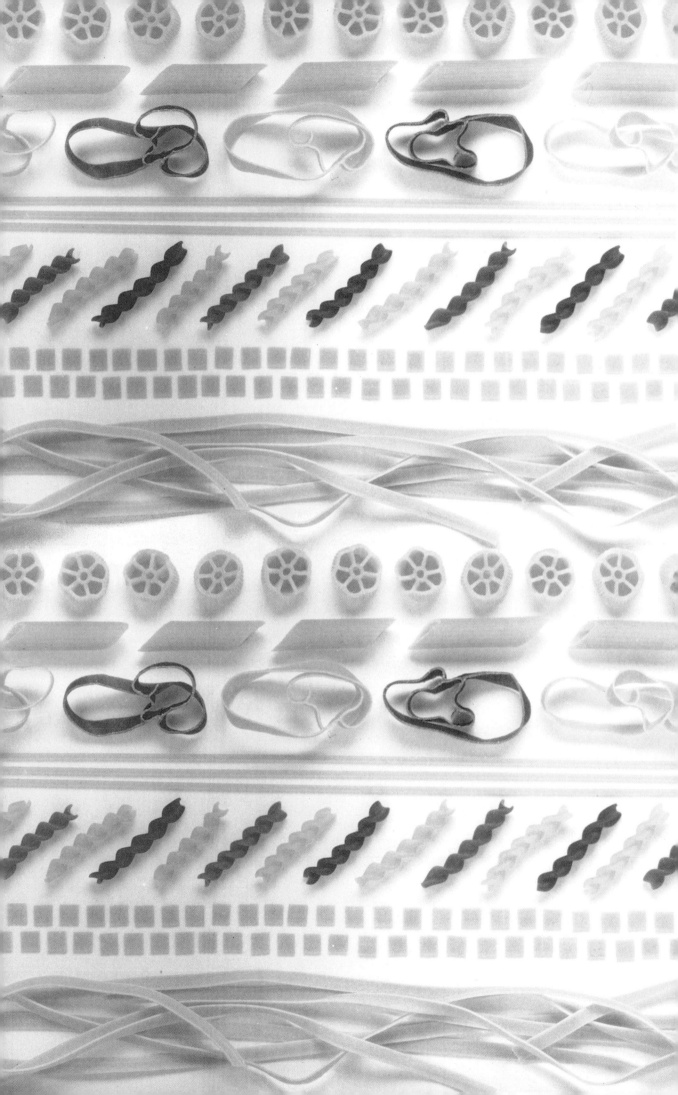